Seen Senr

THE
SCIENCE
OF
HITTING

TED WILLIAMS
AND JOHN UNDERWOOD

A TOUCHSTONE BOOK
PUBLISHED BY SIMON & SCHUSTER

NEW YORK LONDON TORONTO SYDNEY NEW DELHI

Illustrations by Robert Cupp

Photographs on pages 77–81 appear courtesy of Major League Baseball;
except for Boggs, Mattingly and Williams, Focus on Sports Inc.

Touchstone
A Division of Simon & Schuster, Inc.
1230 Avenue of the Americas
New York, NY 10020

First Touchstone trade paperback edition March 2013

TOUCHSTONE and colophon are registered trademarks of Simon & Schuster, Inc.

For information about special discounts for bulk purchases, please contact
Simon & Schuster Special Sales at 1-866-506-1949
or business@simonandschuster.com.

The Simon & Schuster Speakers Bureau can bring authors to your live event.
For more information or to book an event contact the
Simon & Schuster Speakers Bureau at 1-866-248-3049
or visit our website at www.simonspeakers.com.

Designed by Ruth Lee-Mui

Manufactured in the United States of America

37   39   40   38

The Library of Congress has cataloged the previous edition as follows:
Williams, Ted.
The science of hitting.
"A Fireside book."
1. Batting (Baseball) I. Underwood, John, 1934–
II. Title.
GV869.W5   1986   796.357'27   85-31203

ISBN 978-0-671-62103-2

To the young baseball players of America, who dream, as I did, of becoming great hitters.
May this help them on their way.

—TED WILLIAMS

PREFACE

JOHN UNDERWOOD

From the beginning, this was to be a book that would reach, teach, and inspire all ages and levels of play, from high schoolers to collegians, from minor leaguers to big leaguers and anyone anywhere in between who might benefit from an immortal's thoughts on that pivotal part of baseball that he dominated for so many years. He wanted it to be his legacy.

The circumstances of its origin recalls an image of Ted Williams that will stick in my mind for a lifetime, not just for the impact it made but for the depth of feeling—the convictions—of its source.

Williams was discussing his life story that we were shaping for a series in *Sports Illustrated,* later in toto for Simon & Schuster. We had come to this after getting to know each other fishing for tarpon off the Florida Keys, also for the pages of *SI,* the result having prompted the magazine's managing editor to suggest Ted might finally be willing to sit still for a full inspection. He had resisted doing so while he played and for almost a decade after his retirement.

So I asked, and, to my surprise, Williams said yes.

And not long after that, we were poised to begin the process at his home in Islamorada when he stopped me with a caveat, holding up his hand as if to blunt any objections. He said, "I want one whole section of this to be about hitting—my thoughts about hitting a baseball. The conclusions I've reached."

Like what?

"Like the fact that it's the toughest thing to do in sport, where when you get all that attention for being a .300 hitter, it really means you've failed seven out of every ten times you go to bat. Explaining why that is."

And?

"And because there's been a lot of excrement [except he didn't say *excrement*] written about it, stuff that's dead wrong and needs correcting."

Like what?

"Like the fact that it's a slight *up*swing, not a downswing." He stood up to demonstrate, assuming the batter's stance and extending his right hand toward an imaginary pitcher, then sweeping it back along the line a pitch would take coming from the mound.

"The ball angles *down*, not straight or up. You don't need calculus to see it. It's obvious. And it means the best way to hit it is to swing slightly *up*, not level or down. Meet it squarely along its path. They got that wrong for years, ever since Ty Cobb."

He said he even knew what he wanted to title his beliefs on the subject: "The Science of Hitting." Because that's what it is, he said. A science.

He really had it all in his head, down to the illustrations, including one that would require the photographer to lie faceup beneath a clear piece of heavy-duty plastic to capture the Williams swing from underneath. Most especially, he said, he wanted an artist's rendering of the strike zone, filled by equal rows of circles depicting what kind of batting average a player could expect swinging at balls in each of those areas. He said he would supply the figures himself.

And the more he talked, the more we agreed (how could I not?), and the series in *SI* evolved into the book on his life (*My Turn at Bat*) and soon after that, into this one that, I have to say, he probably would have preferred doing in the first place. An avalanche of accolades followed, most notably from big-league players who could best appreciate the depth of his expertise.

But it didn't end there. The eruptions of his passion for the "science" *never* ended. And to fully appreciate that, you have to understand, first, that Ted Williams was a very smart man; that though he barely made it through high school, growing up tough in San Diego, he was smart enough in adulthood to explain in technical terms how the jet engines worked in the fighter planes he'd flown in the Korean war and why a baseball curves when thrown properly.

Hitting one, of course, had been the center of his universe, virtually from childhood. He had said for the autobiography that all he wanted in life "was to walk down the street and hear people say, 'There goes Ted Williams, the greatest hitter who ever lived.'" And whenever it came to the particulars, the ins and outs of hitting, he didn't hesitate to stop a conversation or expand on one to demonstrate.

I have seen him teach specifics to the big-league players he coached or managed—and even those he didn't, like Tony Gwynn, who credited Williams and his instructions in this book for making the difference that put him (Gwynn) in the Hall of Fame. Most impressive for me, however, were the times Ted Williams permitted interruptions of his life to give audience to the younger players who sought him out in almost any imaginable venue, sports or otherwise. They were invariably treated to full-scale renderings of the Williams swing, complete with jarring epithets.

A prime example: Ron Fraser coached the University of Miami baseball team from nowhere to national championship status, and after his first title, Fraser got Ted to come up from Islamorada to bless his players with a "few pointers." The session convened one day before practice by the UM dugout, Ted in the middle with bat in hand making his points. The Miami players were so enthralled that when a bat was accidentally tipped onto the dugout floor, the impact sounded like a car crash. Afterward, Fraser said he had made *The Science of Hitting* required reading.

For Ted Williams, of course, every day was demonstration day. I have been with him when he stood up and perilously rocked the fishing skiff we were in to make a point.

Once, while lounging in a mostly empty hole-in-the-wall restaurant in the Keys (Ted's preference in restaurants were ones in which he didn't have to wear a tie), a mutual friend we had played tennis with made a comment about hitting that Ted jumped up to correct. Grabbing a broom from a nearby corner, he thrust it into the friend's hands and made him swing it to emphasize the point, and never mind the other diners in the room.

But the moment I think says it all—the clincher, if you will—happened in a tent after a long day of hunting for sable antelope on safari in Zambia.

Ted had been named Manager of the Year in his very first season on the job (he had vowed never to do such a silly thing, but the owner of the Washington Senators made him an offer he couldn't refuse). The Senators, a perennial doormat in the American League, had actually won more than they lost. And the reason: in just one spring and summer under Ted's tutelage—often delivered at full volume for all to hear but just as often one-on-one—the Washington hitters had prospered as never before. Every one of the nine players who made up the starting lineup had actually improved their batting averages from the previous season.

The safari in Africa, at the invitation of *The American Sportsman,* was one of the rewards Williams took for himself, and as we settled into our bunks in the tent after that first day, he quietly discussed the Senators' season, recounting some of the hitting glitches he had tried to correct. One player had trouble finding the sweet spots in the strike zone. Another had finally mastered good wrist action. Still another was struggling to get his hips into the swing, etc., etc.

The breaks between Williams's evaluations grew longer and, after an extended silence, I closed my eyes. It had been a tiring day; we were both exhausted. I drifted off.

I don't know how long I was out, but in my half sleep I became aware that Ted was still awake. I opened my eyes to see him standing barefoot in the middle of the tent, his tall, lanky figure outlined against the tent wall by the glow from the campfire outside. He was in that perfect stance, hands clasped together as if holding a bat, swinging away. In his laboratory of a brain, Ted Williams didn't need an audience. With or without my inclusion, he was reviewing one more time his exceptional findings.

Pow. Another perfect swing.

Science, indeed.

THE
SCIENCE
OF
HITTING

The author in his prime

Hitting a baseball—I've said it a thousand times—is the single most difficult thing to do in sport.

I get raised eyebrows and occasional arguments when I say that, but what is there that is harder to do? What is there that requires more natural ability, more physical dexterity, more mental alertness? That requires a greater finesse to go with physical strength, that has as many variables and as few constants, and that carries with it the continuing frustration of knowing that even if you are a .300 hitter—which is a rare item these days—you are going to fail at your job seven out of ten times?

If Joe Montana or Dan Marino completed three of every ten passes they attempted, they would be *ex*-professional quarterbacks. If Larry Bird or Magic Johnson made three of every ten shots they took, their coaches would take the basketball away from them.

Golf? Somebody always mentions golf. You don't have to have good eyesight to play golf. Tommy Armour was a terrific golfer, and he had no sight in one eye. You have to have good eyesight to hit a baseball. Look at the tragedy of Tony Conigliaro of the Red Sox. Six foot three, beautifully developed, strong, aggressive, stylish, and an injured eye ended his career. When I managed the Washington Senators I insisted that Mike Epstein get his eyes checked. He was having difficulties hitting, and I suspected it might be partially due to his vision. He did, and with new contact lenses he had his best season with the Senators. Just a tiny correction.

You don't have to have speed to succeed at golf or great strength or exceptional

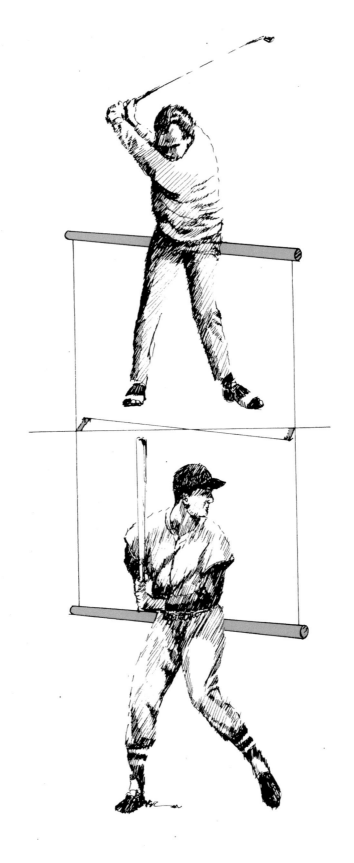

coordination. You don't have to be quick. You don't have to be young. Golfers win major tournaments into their fifties. I hit .316 when I was forty-two years old, and was considered an old, old man in the game.

You never hear a boo in golf. I *know* that's a factor. You don't have a pitcher throwing curves and sliders and knuckleballs, and if he doesn't like you, maybe a fastball at your head. There is nothing to hurt you in golf unless lightning strikes or somebody throws a club. And there's that golf ball, sitting right there for you to hit, and a flat-faced club to hit it with.

Thousands of guys play par golf. Good young golfers swarm into the pros like lemmings. In 1983, the first eleven tournaments on the U.S. tour were won by eleven different players—*the first twenty-three by twenty different players.* Wouldn't it be ironic if Mr. Watson didn't win a tournament all season? Or Mr. Nicklaus? The two biggest names in golf? It could happen. But how many .300 hitters are there? A handful.

I compare golf not to detract from it, because it is a fine game, good fun, sociable, and a game, unlike baseball, you can play for life. There have always been great athletes in golf. Sam Snead comes immediately to mind. There are points of similarity in the swings of the two games—hip action, for one, is a key factor, and the advantage of an inside-out stroke. I will elaborate later.

The thing is, hitting a golf ball has been examined from every angle. Libraries of analysis have been written on the subject and by experts, true experts, like Snead, Armour, Hogan, Nicklaus, and Palmer. I've got their books and I know. There are as many theories as there are tee markers, and for the student a great weight of diagnosis.

Hitting a baseball has had no such barrage of scholarly treatment, and probably that is why there are so many people—even at the big-league level—teaching it incorrectly, or not teaching it at all. Everybody knows how to hit—but very few really do.

The golfer is all ears when it comes to theories. He is receptive to ideas. There is even more to theorize on and to teach in the hitting of a baseball, but there aren't enough qualified guys who do teach it, or enough willingness on the part of the hitters to listen. Then there are the pitching coaches, standing at the batting cage and yelling at the pitchers to "keep it low" or "how's your arm, Lefty? Don't throw too hard, now," and never mind seeing to it that the hitter gets the kind of practice he needs.

Baseball is crying for good hitters. Hitting is the most important part of the game; it is where the big money is, where much of the status is, and the fan interest. The greatest name in American sports history is Babe Ruth, a hitter. I don't know if the story is true or not, but I have to laugh. Ruth was needled one time about the fact that his salary of $80,000 was higher than President Hoover's. Ruth paused a minute and then said, "Well, I had a better year."

DECLINE OF THE HITTER

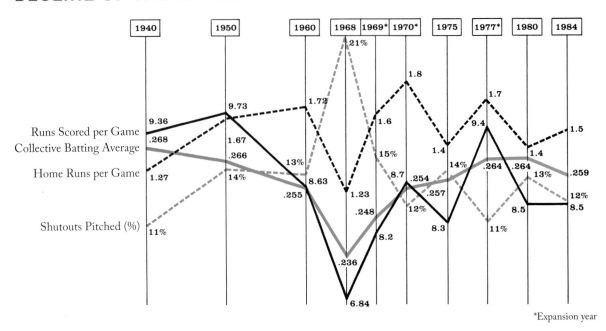

1940	1950	1960	1968	1969*	1970*	1975	1977*	1980	1984

Runs Scored per Game
Collective Batting Average

Home Runs per Game

Shutouts Pitched (%)

*Expansion year

Nowadays a .300-plus power hitter like a Mays or a Clemente or an Aaron or a Frank Robinson can make a million dollars or more. Into that category now would be George Brett of the Royals, Eddie Murray of the Orioles, Dale Murphy of the Braves, Don Mattingly of the Yankees, and Wade Boggs of the Red Sox. For an outfielder, hitting is 75 percent of his worth, in most cases more important than fielding and arm and speed combined. Terry Moore was a great fielder. Dom DiMaggio was a great fielder. Nobody played the outfield any better than Jimmy Piersall. But when it comes down to it, the guys people remember are the hitters.

Yet today there does not seem to be a player in baseball who is going to wind up a lifetime .333 hitter, although Rod Carew will be close. Wade Boggs has made a terrific impression in his first four years, but it's a little early to tell with him. Hank Aaron finished his career at .305, Roberto Clemente at .317, Willie Mays at .302, Al Kaline at .297, and Frank Robinson at .304. Mickey Mantle, as great as he was, was unable to finish above .300.

In the years from 1950 to 1968, Major League batting averages, figured as a whole, dropped 30 points—from .266 to .236. They have risen again since then, I think mainly because of two expansions (in 1969 and 1977), which invariably water down the pitching and makes it easier for the hitters for a while. There were fewer home runs hit per game (1.23) in 1968 than there had been in twenty years. Runs scored per game dropped from 9.73 to 6.84, the lowest in sixty years. Batting averages and runs scored began going up again in 1968 and 1970 when four new teams were added to the big leagues. There were pitchers in the big leagues who other years were not good enough to be there, just as it happened again when two teams were added in 1977.

A further help to the hitters was the lowering of the mound from 15 inches to 10. Nobody made a big thing about it, but the ball was hopped up a little, too. Unfortunately, so was the thinking. I heard a lot of talk during that period about the "advantage" of the so-called down swing, which has never been good batting technique. I'll get to that later.

The longer season is blamed for the decline in hitting, and the pitching overall is supposed to be better. Logistics are definitely a factor— the increase in night games, the size of the new parks (Chavez Ravine in Los Angeles is a pasture compared to cozy old Ebbets Field), the disturbed routine of cross-country travel that forces you to eat different hours, sleep differently. Certainly a week should be cut off both ends of the season for no other reason than to get away from some of that lousy cold weather. It's hard to hit in cold weather. But I wonder. If it were the longer season, you would expect the better hitters to average higher—.360, .370, or better—for at least 100 games, but only one or two have been able to do so. When the season's only a couple months old, neither league will have ten guys hitting .300.

How, too, can the pitching be better when there are fewer pitchers in organized baseball (fewer leagues, fewer everything, actually)? When expansion has made starters out of sixty or more who would otherwise still be in the minor leagues?

After four years of managing the Washington Senators/Texas Rangers, the one big impression I got was that the game hadn't changed. Except maybe now because of what the artificial surfaces are doing to it, it's basically the same as it was when I played. I see the same type pitchers, the same type hitters. But after fifty years of watching it I'm more convinced than ever that there aren't as many good hitters in the game, guys who can whack the ball around when it's over the plate, guys like Aaron and Clemente and Frank Robinson. There are plenty of guys with power, guys who hit the ball a long way, but I see so many who lack finesse, who should hit for average but don't.

The answers are not all that hard to figure. They talked for years about the ball being dead. The ball isn't dead; the hitters are, from the neck up. Everybody's trying to *pull* the ball, to begin with. Almost everybody from the left fielder to the utility shortstop is trying to hit home runs, which is folly, and I will tell you why as we go along—and how Ted Williams, that notorious pull hitter, learned for himself.

I will probably get carried away and sound like Al Simmons and Ty Cobb sounded to me when they used to cart their criticism of my hitting into print. I don't mean to criticize individuals here. Not at all. I do criticize these trends.

I think hitting can be improved at almost any level, and my intention is to show how, and what I think it takes to be a good hitter, even a .400 hitter if the conditions are ever right again—from the theory to the mechanics to the application.

If I can help somebody, fine. That's the whole idea. I feel in my heart that nobody in this game ever devoted more concentration to the batter's box than Theodore Samuel Williams, a guy who practiced until the blisters bled, and loved doing it, and got more delight out of examining by conversation and observation the art of hitting the ball. If that does not qualify me, nothing will.

HOW THE HITTERS IMPROVED UNDER TED WILLIAMS

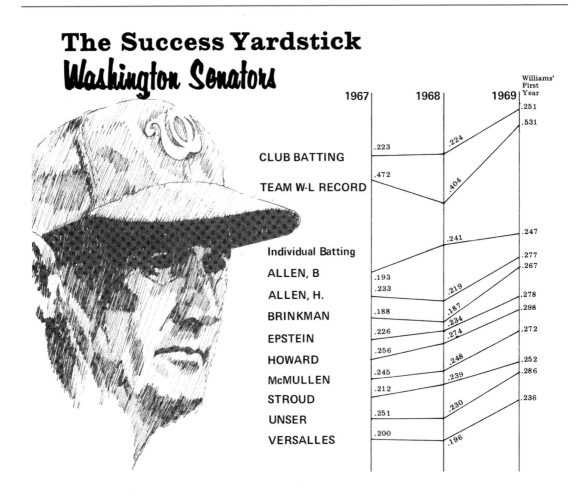

I have to admit to a pride in the results we got with the Senators my first year. The fun I had was seeing them improve and realizing they could win, and some of them did make dramatic turnarounds. Eddie Brinkman, who I knew from the beginning was a better hitter than his record indicated, jumped from .187 to .266. Del Unser went from .230 to .286, Hank Allen .219 to .278, Ken McMullen .248 to .272. Frank Howard hit .296 and Mike Epstein .278, the best years they ever had in the big leagues. That was tremendous satisfaction to me.

If there is such a thing as a science in sport, hitting a baseball is it. As with any science, there are fundamentals, certain tenets of hitting every good batter or batting coach could tell you. But it is not an exact science. Much of it has been poorly defined, or not defined at all, and some things have been told wrong for years.

The consequence is a collection of mistaken ideas that batters parrot around. I know because I'm as guilty as the next guy.

The "level swing," for example, has always been advocated. I used to believe it, and I used to say the same thing. But the ideal swing is *not* level, and it's not *down,* and I'll tell you why as we get to it. I'll also tell you why wrist "snap" is overrated—and how wrong you are if you think you hit the ball with rolling wrists (as in golf). And I'll also tell you why left-handed pull hitter T. S. Williams does not think a pulled ball is something to strive for, and why he may have been a better left-hand

hitter if he had not been a natural *right-hander.*

HITTER, KNOW YOURSELF

It would be nice to be able to lay down some hard rules that would eliminate all weaknesses for a batter. Every batter has some; and every pitcher, his natural enemy, is on the lookout; though pitchers as a breed are dumb and hardheaded. The smart ones like Whitey Ford and Bob Feller and Ed Lopat are always after an edge.

I remember the 1949 All-Star game in Brooklyn. Lou Boudreau of Cleveland was managing the American League team. An astute guy. The National League pitcher that day was Larry Jansen. He threw me a slow curve and I pulled it foul, another slow curve and I pulled it foul, then he busted one right in on the fists and I took it. Strike three.

I'd been wearing out Cleveland that year, even with Boudreau's shift stacking the defense to the right side, and they didn't know what to do with me. After the All-Star game, they had this meeting. Jim Bagby, who had been traded from our club, told me about it later. He said Boudreau told him to try Jansen's method. Bagby had good control. Sure enough, we're in Boston and Bagby throws me a slow curve and I pull it foul. Another slow curve, foul again. Now a fastball inside, and I hit it in the seats. As Bagby tells it, when he came to the bench he said to Boudreau, "That is *not* the way to pitch to that guy." The point, of course, is that you can't beat a good hitter with the same pitch every time.

I think you will find as we go along that much of what I have to say about hitting is self-education—thinking it out, learning the situations, knowing your opponent, and most important, knowing yourself. Lefty O'Doul was a great hitter, one of the prettiest I ever saw, and he always said that most hitting faults came from a lack of knowledge, uncertainty, and fear—and that boils down to knowing yourself. You, the hitter, are the greatest variable in this game, because to know yourself takes dedication.

Today that's a hard thing to have. Today ballplayers have a dozen distractions. They're always on the run. In the old days we didn't fly, we rode the train. We might be ten to twelve hours on a train, and much of the talk was hitting. The men I played for, and with, inspired that kind of thing. Joe Cronin especially. He was a wonderful manager for a hitter because he was always getting guys roused up, getting them thinking and talking about it, challenging them with questions. Rogers Hornsby was like that in Minneapolis, and Lefty O'Doul when I was a kid on the Coast.

I suppose the Washington and Texas players I managed would say I was like that. When I came around, they wanted to talk hitting because they knew I was interested, because they knew I would have something to contribute. Stan Musial always said whenever he and I got together we talked hitting, because we both enjoyed it, and there were players like Kaline and Rocky Colovito who were generous with their praise for the times I tried to help them. The thing is, I *did* enjoy it, and it was that way with me from the time I was a young player.

We didn't have television, we didn't have a lot of money to play around with. A complete baseball atmosphere. We talked, we experimented, we swapped bats. I was forever trying a new stance, trying to hit like Greenberg or Foxx or somebody, and then going back to my old way. I recommend that for kids. Experiment. Try what you see that looks good on somebody else. Try different bats, a bigger handle, a bigger barrel, anything.

LIGHT, BUT RIGHT

My preference was a light bat. I treated my bats like they were special, keeping them usable as long as possible. I boned them to get the fibers together. I didn't want them chipped or discolored, because those are distractions. Just like the uniform—I didn't want the cap too tight or the pants bagging or the sleeves flapping. I didn't want any distractions. I often swung with the label down so I couldn't see it for just that reason.

When we started using pine tar, or resin and oil, on the handles to improve the grip, most of the players let it stay on a week or more before scrubbing it off for a fresh coat, but I cleaned my bats with alcohol every night. I took them to the post office to check their weights. Finally I got the Red Sox to put a scale in the clubhouse. I wanted them checked because bats pick up condensation and dirt lying around on the ground. They can gain an ounce or more in a surprisingly short time.

I ordered 35-inch bats, narrow-grained, medium barrel, weighing 33 ounces, but they'd come 33 ½, or 34, so I always double-checked. After a while, I changed the order to read not *over* 33 ounces. I'll never forget when John Hillerich of Hillerich and Bradsby, the Louisville Slugger Company, put six bats on a bed one time. One was a half ounce heavier than the others. He had me close my eyes and pick the heavier bat. I picked it out twice in a row.

Bat lengths, shapes, and weights will vary according to preference. Ty Cobb said he used a 40-ounce bat, but was down to a 35-ouncer near the end of his career. Too, Cobb choked up on the bat. Choke up 2 inches on a 36-ounce bat and it feels like a 34-ouncer. George Sisler had a 38–42 ounce range. Lefty O'Doul's weighed 36 ounces. Musial's were 32–33. Babe Ruth, according to Hillerich and Bradsby, had a fantastic variance of sizes and they were all heavy—40 to 54 ounces. But Ruth himself was a big, burly guy, and for a string bean like me—6 foot 3, 190 pounds at the top of my game in 1950—lighter bats made more sense. I see no percentage at all in using a heavy bat. You can get the same result by being quicker with a light bat.

I switched to a light bat as early as 1938, when I was with Minneapolis, the year before I went up with the Red Sox. It was in late August, and the weather was awful—hotter than I had ever seen it on the West Coast. I was having my first real good year in professional baseball, leading the American Association in batting, home runs, runs batted in, everything. But I was on base so much, swinging and running and sweating, that I felt wrung out.

One night we were in Columbus, another hot muggy night, and I happened to pick up one of Stan Spence's bats. What a light bat. A toothpick, the lightest in the rack. It was real pumpkin wood, too. You could see imprints all over it where the balls had hit. But it felt good in my hands—I'd been swinging a 35-ouncer—so I asked Stan if I could use it.

First time up, bases loaded, a little left-hander pitching, and the count went to 3 and 2. As I usually did in those cases, I choked up and said to myself, "I'm not going to strike out now, I'm going to get some wood on that ball," and he threw me a good pitch, low and away but just over the plate. I gave this bat a little flip, and I could hardly believe it—a home run to center field. Not the longest poke in the world, only 410 feet, but long enough.

That woke me up. I said to myself, "Gee, the lightest bat I ever used, and I hit a ball like that." Fifteen or twenty years ago everybody started making a big fuss about how the power hitters—Mantle, Killebrew, Mays—were using light bats, but I was using a light bat way back then, and I *always* used light bats from then on. I kept six or seven bats ready all the time, some as light as 32 ounces, but never over 34 ounces.

I say never. My last really outstanding season was in 1957, when, as an old man pushing forty, I hit .388—a half-dozen hits short of .400. In the spring that year I had used a little heavier bat, 34 ½ ounces. I choked up on it about a quarter an inch, and, boy, the balls were flying around, a lot of sharp hits, all over the lot.

I liked the bat so much I started the season with it, and right away I was getting hits into the spaces they opened for me in left field when they used that tough shift. I wasn't getting around quite as fast with the heavier bat, but against the shift it was perfect.

After a while, when they started to think—this guy's getting old, he can't pull anymore—and began spreading out more, I switched back to a lighter model. By the middle of the summer when I always hit well I was pulling them into right field again.

THINK ABOUT IT

In my twenty-two years of professional baseball, I went to bat almost 8,000 times, and every trip to the plate was an adventure, one that I could remember and store up as information. I honestly believe I can recall everything there was to know about my first 300 home runs—who the pitcher was, the count, the pitch itself, where the ball landed. I didn't have to keep a written book on pitchers—I *lived* a book on pitchers.

I tried to do that with the Senators and Rangers. Make guys think, even the guys on the bench whose interest might otherwise lag. Where was the pitch that Frank Howard hit? What was it? Curveball? Slider? Ask the guys on the bench, the pitchers, everybody. Get in the game, know what's going on, know the reason when that pitcher takes the bread out of your mouth. That makes sense to me.

And then to practice, practice, practice. I said I hit until the blisters bled, and I did; it was something I forced myself to do to build up those hard, tough calluses. I doubt you'd see as many calluses today. Most players hit with those golf gloves, to begin with, but more important, they don't take as much batting practice—as much *extra* batting practice, and that's how you learn. Part of the problem is there just isn't enough time. It used to be we'd have thirty-three or thirty-four players practicing in the spring; today it's more like forty-five. A guy doesn't get in the batting cage often enough and doesn't stay there long enough. You see it even in the Little Leagues. With all the regimentation they get, and all the emphasis on playing games instead of practicing, a kid isn't afforded the time he needs in the batting cage.

As a player I used to complain all the time about it: "Look at Snead and Hogan and those other golfers, they're out there hitting practice balls forever. I'm lucky if I can get fifteen practice swings a day. If I could get an hour's batting practice every day I could hit .450." I was exaggerating, of course, but that's how eager I was.

I was a pain in the neck asking the older guys about pitchers. I was *always* asking about pitchers: What kind of pitcher is Bobo Newsom? What kind of pitcher is Red Ruffing? What about Tommy Bridges? Ted Lyons? Lefty Gomez? Schoolboy Rowe? I wanted the information, and I wanted to put it to use. I remember when Ken Chase came to our club from the Senators. He was a tough left-hander with a good curve, and I'd had a hard time hitting him. When he joined us, I got him to come out and pitch to me every morning before a game. This went on for several weeks, and the way he tells it, one day I yelled out to him, "Okay, buddy, I can hit you with my eyes shut now."

Tris Speaker had a player like that when he was managing Cleveland in the 1920s—shortstop Joe Sewell. Sewell had replaced Ray Chapman when Chapman was killed by a pitched ball, and the book on Sewell was he couldn't hit a left-hand curve. So he got left-handers to throw him curveball after curveball in practice. Every day the same thing. He wound up hitting .300 or better seven years in a row. That's the kind of dedication I'm talking about.

HIT ACCORDING TO YOUR STYLE

Hitting a baseball—I've said this a thousand times, too—is 50 percent from the neck up, and the more we talk about it the more you'll see why that is so. The other 50 percent is *hitting according to your style.* Except when something is radically wrong, you won't find me doing much to alter a player's style. Chances are you won't even hear me talk about it. Everybody talks fundamentals—arms, feet, legs, etc.—but I seldom do.

I like to demonstrate the necessary ingredients of a good swing, because there is logic in using them in the optimum way, but there are a dozen deviations from the norm: the size of the bat can make a difference, choking up can make a difference, moving away from the plate, moving closer—things dependent on an individual and his makeup. Show me ten great hitters and I'll show you ten different styles—Ty Cobb with his hands apart, Joe DiMaggio with his extra wide stance, Hank Greenberg with his bat flattened out, Stan Musial all coiled up in the back of the batter's box.

There were, as far as I'm concerned, two great pieces of advice given me early in my career. One was from Rogers Hornsby, when I was with Minneapolis the year before I went to the big leagues. He told me the single most important thing for a hitter was "to get a good ball to hit." The other was given me when I needed it most, as a kid starting out at San Diego in the Pacific Coast League, cocky as they come but not really sure of myself, and it came from Lefty O'Doul, to my mind one of the great hitters of all time. He said, "Son, whatever you do, don't let anybody change you." Your style is your own.

Now, there are all kinds of hitting styles. The style must fit the player, not the other way around. It is not a Williams or a DiMaggio or a Ruth method. It is a matter of applying certain truths of hitting to a player's natural makeup. If you've got a natural talent to work with, you sure don't try to take anything away from him. You add to what he already has, or you suggest a little adjustment.

For example, when Carl Yastrzemski, who had been great in the minors, first came up he was wheeling the bat all around his neck. I was with the Red Sox in the spring then and I spoke to Carl. I didn't make a big thing of it, I just tried to impress him with this: "Don't forget, Carl, the pitching in this league is going to be a little faster. You have to be a little quicker. You can't have any lost motion." I didn't tell him to *stop* doing anything. I didn't want him to think that much about it. He worked it out for himself.

Much of your style will depend on your size and strength and will determine how pitchers pitch to you. You adopt and adjust accordingly. When I managed the Senators, I had a skinny little shortstop named Eddie Brinkman, barely 170 pounds and always pitched to a lot differently, say, than Frank Howard, who was 6 foot 7, 270 pounds and hit the ball a ton. Brinkman didn't have to be as smart a hitter as Howard, because Brinkman was going to be made to hit by the pitchers he faced. A pitcher facing Brinkman says to himself, "Don't walk this little guy, he gets 160 hits a year and 140 are singles, so why walk him and eliminate the chance to get him out by making him hit?" Hitting .270 means he's still only going to hit 2.7 out of 10, so why walk him? On the other

hand, good hitters today like a Murphy or a Murray or a Mattingly or a Mike Schmidt of the Phillies can hurt you with a long ball, so the pitchers want to be much more careful with them. As a rule, they have to be smarter hitters.

Brinkman had his best season for us in 1969 because he made some adjustments, and I was given credit for those adjustments and deserve none. He had already picked out a bottle bat he could handle better and was choking way up on it when I saw him in the spring. He asked me what I thought, and I said, "Well, it's all right," but I said to myself as far up as he was choking that bat I hope he doesn't hit himself in the belly with it.

You could see in Brinkman the eagerness you want in a player. The first time I saw him in the batting cage, all eager and alive, I said if he was a .180 hitter I'd eat an alligator. It didn't take a genius to see that. As it turned out, he didn't have a great lifetime average when he retired in 1975, but in those two years with me he hit .266 and .262, and I was proud of him. The only thing I tried to impress on Brinkman was to be quicker with the bat, and to get the ball on the ground when hitting to the opposite field. The tendency to the opposite field is to be late, and when you're late, you're swinging under the ball and more likely to pop it up.

It didn't do a guy like Brinkman any good to hit the ball in the air because ninety-nine times out of a hundred his best shot in the air is not going out of the park. Hit a ball on the ground and it's a tougher play, things can happen. Brinkman worked at it—he worked on the inside-out swing, enabling him to hit more to right field, and I want to tell you that little guy got big hits all year for us. I'd just as soon see Brinkman up there in a tight spot as anybody. He made the most of his style.

Now, when the mistakes are mental, and the vast majority of them are, a coach has to bear down. I remember a chat with Rico Petrocelli a few years ago. I said, "Rico, have I ever told you anything about hitting?"

"No."

I said, "You know why? Because I can't. You have a wonderful style. You hit pretty near every pitch well. You've got good power. In a jam, I'd as soon see you at the plate as anybody. But you know what, Rico? I'm beginning to think you're stupid. You don't even have the vaguest idea what is going on at the plate. Just yesterday a guy threw a fastball right by you on a 3-and-1 pitch."

What I meant was that here was a kid who with two strikes could very well hit as tough a pitch as you could throw, but when he had you in the hole 2-and-0 or 3-and-1, and you *had* to come right down the middle with it, he did not realize that he could really rip, really take advantage of the edge. He was up there looking for a tough one when he could have been taking pickings. Getting his pitch—just like batting practice. I had to laugh. Rico said, "You know, Ted, you're right. I'm stupid."

It's not really so complicated. It's a matter of being observant, of learning through trial and error, of picking up things. You watch a pitcher warm up, and you see everything's high, or his breaking ball is in the dirt. If he isn't getting the breaking ball over you can think about waiting for the fastball. Or if he's *making* you hit the breaking ball, you can lay for it.

You think of the count, the game situation. You remember the series before, the way he worked. You can be sure if he got you out on a bad ball he'll be coming back with it. What Mattingly or Murphy or Dave Winfield do this year will have a bearing on how the pitchers pitch to them next year. These are the things that fall in line.

Now, you can sit on the bench, pick your nose, scratch your bottom, and it all goes by, and you're the loser. The observant guy will get the edge. He'll take advantage of every opening. I was known as a hitter who "guessed" a lot, and I will get into that and why I advocate it, but for me guessing was observing. Observing that you can pick up some guys' curveball the moment they throw it, the way they have to really snap it off to get it going. And knowing what you've swung at, knowing the pitch you hit or missed. Knowing the pitcher's pattern.

It dumbfounded me when a batter couldn't tell what he had hit. Bobby Doerr was like that. Doerr was a solid .280 hitter, but he'd come back to the bench and I'd say, "What was the pitch?" "I dunno. Curve, I think," even when he'd hit a home run.

Nothing pleased me more than to get a

second chance at a pitcher who got me out on something he thought had fooled me. I couldn't *wait* to get up again, because I knew he would throw it again. My last home run, my last time at bat in the big leagues in 1960, was off Jack Fisher of Baltimore, who had thrown a fastball by me for the second strike. He tried to do it again on the next pitch.

The better professional golfers are thinking all the time. I'm sure if you asked Tom Watson if he had to hit a five-iron through a twenty-five-mile crosswind, how much draw he'd have to put on it to make it drift to the target, he could tell you exactly how much. It wasn't just his physical ability, it was his devotion to practice, his concentration, his observation. And in order to excel a hitter has to have those things.

No hitter has it all. There probably never has been what you would call the "complete" hitter. Ruth struck out more than he should have. Cobb didn't have the power, he didn't have great style. Harry Heilmann wasn't serious enough. Shoeless Joe Jackson must have come close because all the old-time hitters used to talk about how great he was, how complete a hitter he was, but of all the hitters I saw—if I had to name one guy—I suppose it would be Rogers Hornsby. Hornsby was the closest to the complete hitter—style, power, smartness, everything.

I'll never forget as a twenty-year-old kid in camp with the Minneapolis team at Daytona Beach, standing around the batting cage or in the lobby of the hotel, picking Hornsby's brains for everything I could, even personal things I had no right knowing: How much money did you lose at the track? How much did you bet? And he'd stay out there with me every day *after* practice and we'd have hitting contests, just the two of us, and that old rascal would just keeping zinging those line drives.

Hornsby used to say, "A great hitter isn't born, he's made. He's made out of practice, fault correction, and confidence." Hornsby was talking about himself, I think. He had a lot of confidence. He wasn't a very diplomatic guy. He'd come right out and say things, whatever was on his mind. If the owner of the club said something about baseball he didn't like, Hornsby would just say, "What the hell do you know about it?" But he knew what it took to hit.

THREE RULES TO HIT BY

There are three things I would emphasize to any hitter before even considering the rudiments of a good swing. These three things are more constant than the swing itself, and every bit as important, and the first is something Rogers Hornsby originally impressed on me that spring long ago: *To get a good ball to hit.* The first rule in the book.

The second is something you must always take up there with you: *proper thinking.* Have you done your homework? What's this guy's best pitch? What did he get you out on last time? I remember one time Hal Newhouser of Detroit dusted me off, then struck me out on three pitches, the last one a sharp letter-high fastball. When I came back to the bench I was livid. Rip Russell made a crack, and I said, "Listen, I'll bet five bucks if he throws that same pitch again, I'll hit it out." Newhouser did, and I did.

The third thing is *to be quick with the bat*. It applies all the time, and I'll tell you ways to increase your quickness.

But what about that "good ball to hit?" You can see in the strike zone picture (see page 25) what I considered my happy areas, where I consistently hit the ball hard for high averages, and the areas graded down to those spots I learned to lay off, especially that low pitch on the outside 3 ½ inches of the plate. Ty Cobb once said, "Ted Williams sees more of the ball than any man alive—but he demands a perfect pitch. He takes too many bases on balls."

I didn't resent that. I'm sure Cobb thought he was right. What is "seeing"? I had 20–10 vision. A lot of guys can see that well. I sure couldn't read labels on revolving phonograph records as people wrote I did. I couldn't "see" the bat hit the ball, another thing they wrote, but I knew by the feel of it. A good carpenter doesn't have to see the head of the hammer strike the nail but he still hits it square every time.

What I had more of wasn't eyesight, it was discipline, and isn't it funny? I took so many "close" pitches I wound up, at the time of my retirement, third in all-time bases-loaded home runs, among the top five in all-time home runs, in the top three in runs batted in per time at bat, and I drove in more than a

fifth of the Red Sox runs in my twenty years in Boston. I averaged .344 for a career.

I had a higher percentage of game-winning home runs than Ruth, I was second only to Ruth in slugging and percentage combined; I was walked more frequently than Ruth and struck out less—once every eleven times up to Ruth's one in six. I had to be doing something right, and for my money the principal something was being selective.

I have said that a good hitter can hit a pitch that is over the plate three times better than a great hitter with a questionable ball in a tough spot. Pitchers still make enough mistakes to give you some in your happy zone. But the greatest hitter living can't hit bad balls good.

Sure, you get occasional base hits on pitches in the gray areas; Yogi Berra and Joe Medwick were so-called bad ball hitters, usually on high or inside pitches. A high ball can sometimes be a good ball to hit if it's close to that area you hit well in. But more often than not, you hit a bad pitch in a tough spot and nothing happens. Nothing. And when you start fishing for the pitch that's an inch off the plate, the pitcher—if he's smart—will put the next one *2* inches off. Then *3*. And before you know it you're making fifty outs a year on pitches you never should have swung at.

Giving the pitcher an extra 2 inches around the strike zone increases the area of the strike zone 35 percent. Don't believe it? My strike zone, almost to the inch, was 22 by 32, or 4.8 square feet. Add 2 inches all around and it becomes 26 by 36, a total of 6.5 square feet—35 percent more area for the pitcher to work on. Give a Major League pitcher that kind of advantage and he'll murder you.

Now, if a .250 hitter up forty times gets ten hits, maybe if he had laid off bad pitches he would have gotten five walks. That's five fewer at bats, or ten hits for 35, or .286. And he would have scored more—everybody has been crying for more runs—because he would have been on base more.

SMARTER IS BETTER

Frank Howard of the Senators had that kind of problem. He hit a lot of home runs, he's the strongest man I've ever seen in baseball, but he wasn't getting on base nearly as often as he should. He struck out a lot, he swung at bad pitches, he swung big all the time.

It's funny, really, because everybody seemed to know about it but Howard. I was in Africa one winter, on a hunting trip, and a missionary came up to me in a dime store in Nairobi and asked me if Frank Howard was "still swinging from his heels at everything." That ought to tell you how obvious it was. Well, it was obvious to me the first time I saw him play, when he was with the Dodgers in a World Series in 1963. I knew then exactly what I would say to him if I ever got the chance: the value of knowing the strike zone. The value of proper thinking at the plate. The importance of getting a good ball to hit. Of knowing when not to be too big with his swing.

We talked about it many times, my first spring with Washington, and I think the more we talked, the more sense it made to him. Howard's a smart guy, and he works hard. We analyzed his bases on balls: only 54 in 1968, and 12 of those were intentional. The *lead*-off batter should get 40 walks. Howard didn't know the strike zone. It was as simple as that.

Halfway through the 1969 season he had almost as many walks as he drew the entire previous season. He wound up with 102 and cut his strikeouts by a third. His average was higher than ever, he scored more runs, and he *still* hit more home runs, some of them out of sight. In 1970 he led the league in home runs (45) and RBIs (140) and walked 130 times. Still improving.

After pitchers find out you're not going to bite at bad balls, they have to make a choice: give you a better pitch or pitch around you. Phil Rizzuto said that Joe McCarthy, when he was managing the Yankees, told his pitchers to pitch around me, to walk me, and take a chance on the next batter. Casey Stengel was supposed to have said the same thing. According to Tom Sturdivant, it was an automatic fine for the Yankee pitcher if I beat them in the seventh, eighth, or ninth inning.

Your opportunities then depend a lot on who is batting behind you, and you'll have to exercise some patience. If you're Babe Ruth you had Lou Gehrig behind you, so you got your share of opportunities. When I had Junior Stephens hitting behind me and he was at the top of his game, we had a great thing going. Other times it wasn't quite so good.

The year before Mickey Mantle quit, I read

where he said, "I don't get the good balls to hit I used to." Why? Because Mantle was the guy they pitched around, and as it happens the Yankee lineup wasn't loaded with good hitters before and behind Mantle as it had been.

The mistake Mantle would have made would have been to start going for bad pitches, because then he'd be no better than the .250 hitter.

I don't claim I never walked to first base on a 3–2 pitch without saying, "Gee, I wish I'd hit that first strike." But for some reason I didn't. Either I was looking for something else, or it fooled me—and when a pitch fools you and you've got less than two strikes, *take it. Take it.*

A hitter learns in time where his happy zones are. There isn't a hitter living who can hit a high ball as well as he can a low, or vice versa, or outside as well as inside. All hitters have areas they like to hit in. But you can't beat the fact that you've *got* to get a good ball to hit.

It's very likely that once you've made yourself sensitive to the strike zone, you'll be a little more conscious of what you think are bad calls by the umpire. But don't waste your time arguing with umpires. Number one, you can't do anything about it. Two, they're not that far wrong the majority of the time.

I would say umpires are capable of calling a ball within an inch of where it is. As a hitter, I felt I could tell within a half inch. There is no question that some strikes are called balls, and some balls are called strikes, but you're far better off forgetting the calls that hurt you and concentrating on that next pitch or that next turn at bat.

If you've struck out on a ball you thought was bad, don't argue. Talk to a teammate, somebody you know pays as much attention to the game as you do. Ask him if the ball was low or outside or wherever you thought it was, and if he agrees with the umpire, file it in your memory. You've got some work to do on that particular pitch. You might even make a diagram for yourself to pinpoint the problem areas. Paul Waner did that, and I did it.

I gave the pitcher the outer 2 or 3 inches of the plate on pitches over the low-outside corner—up to two strikes. (On the third strike you can't take that pitch.) As you can see from my chart, they were the toughest for me, partly because of the strength I had lost in my left arm when I splintered the elbow against the fence in Comiskey Park during the 1950 All-Star game.

Up until then I was confident there was no way a pitcher could get me out consistently. They had an article in one of the magazines one year, quoting pitchers on how they pitched to Mantle and me. Bob Lemon said his sinker was the best weapon against Williams. Dick Donovan said he would challenge me with fastballs. Jim Bunning said he hadn't figured out a way to fool me but that he could get Mantle to chase a bad ball once in a while. Billy Pierce said he hoped for "minimum damage" and that he varied his pitches as much as possible—sliders, fastballs, slow-breaking stuff, and prayers.

Bunning said, "One day I pitched him outside, then low, then fast, then a curve, and finally a slider. Williams hit a home run, and I thought it was a helluva pitch."

What they all were saying was that there was no accurate book on me, and that's what a batter strives for, but the fact is that the low-outside pitch was tough on me after I hurt the elbow. I was 25 percent weaker in that arm, and you need your outside arm for that pitch. So I laid off it as much as I could or when the pitcher was throwing balloons. I was still in position to hit it. Some guys stand so deep in the box they don't have a chance on a pitch curving over that low-outside corner. (Stan Musial might be considered an exception to the rule—he stood deep in the box, but he had a long sweep to his swing, a long stride, and big arc, and could handle that pitch.) After a while they all pitched me there. Or tried to.

GUESS? YES!

"Proper thinking" is 50 percent of effective hitting, and it is more than just doing your homework on a pitcher or studying the situation in a game. It is "anticipating," too, when you are at the plate, and a lot of hitters will say that is college talk for "guessing" and some will be heard to say in a loud voice, "Don't do it!" They're wrong. Guessing, or anticipating, goes hand in hand with proper thinking.

A simple example: If a pitcher is throwing fastballs and curves and only the fastballs are in the strike zone, you would be silly to look for a curve, wouldn't you?

Sam Rice was a great outfielder for the Senators in the 1920s and 30s, with a lifetime average of .322. Joe Cronin always said he should have been in the Hall of Fame years ago, but he finally made it in 1963, and when I went with Washington in 1969 I got a chance to talk with Rice at a banquet. He said, "Ted, I always wanted to ask you. Did you guess at the plate?"

"Did I guess?" I said. "Boy, I guess I did!"

He was delighted. "I knew it," he said. "I knew it. I go around asking these young hitters today if they guess at the plate, and they say no because somewhere along the line somebody has told them 'Don't guess.' And the funny thing is they're all hitting .230."

Well, you've got to guess, you've got to have an idea. All they ever write about the good hitters is what great reflexes they have, what great style, what strength, what quickness, but never how smart the guy is at the plate, and that's 50 percent of it. From the ideas come the "proper thinking," and the "anticipation," the "guessing."

I am sure one reason I became a good hitter was that I was exposed to the word early. At eighteen I might not have been quite as strong as I was at twenty-eight or thirty-eight, but I had better eyesight, better reflexes, could run faster, etc. But at seventeen or eighteen I wasn't thinking as clearly at the plate as I was later on. When I came up with San Diego in 1937, I hit .271, then .291. My average went up steadily thereafter because in those formative years I was exposed to experienced players who knew the game between the pitcher and batter. The same was true for Joe DiMaggio because the Pacific Coast League in those days had a lot of older players—thirty-four, thirty-six, thirty-eight years old—experienced guys who played in the big leagues and were back down, guys who could tell a youngster something.

I'd hound them for advice, and they'd talk to me: "What'd you go out on, kid?" "Well, that little curve . . ." "All right, next time lay for it." Elementary equations at first, but awakening in me the knowledge that there was more to hitting than taking a bat up to the plate.

Obviously, you don't just "guess" curve or "guess" fastball. You work from a frame of reference, you learn what you might expect in certain instances, and you guess from there. Certainly you won't guess a pitch the pitcher can't get over; he might have a terrific curve, but if he can't get it over, forget it. Certainly the pitch you anticipate when the count is 0 and 2 (a curveball, probably, if the pitcher has one) is not the pitch you anticipate when the count is 2 and 0 (fastball, almost without exception). Certainly if you are the kind of impatient hitter who will swing at anything at any time, you will do yourself no good guessing at all because with that kind of latitude a pitcher will throw you nothing good to hit.

But if you have developed discipline at the plate, and can wait for that good ball to hit, you have a right to think along with the pitcher, and you will surprise yourself how often you outguess him.

To cure a problem, or to beat a problem pitch, "anticipating" can be invaluable. We have a player on our Washington club who had trouble with high fastballs and inside fastballs. He couldn't get around on them. We shortened his bat, we lightened his bat. He wouldn't accept choking up on it because he's a big strong guy, but we tried everything to get him to open up quicker, to be quicker with the bat. Nothing worked. The word was out on him.

So we started talking to him about *anticipating* the fastball, about looking for it high inside. Still he had trouble. Finally I said, "All right,—, I want you to *start* your swing inside, or *start* your swing high before you even know it's going to be there, and if it's not there, hold up, *take* the pitch." When he did that, he started crashing a few.

I used to have to do the same thing with Virgil Trucks of the Tigers, a great fastball pitcher. If I just said to myself, "I'll watch for the fastball," and waited for it, I didn't get the results I wanted. I had to anticipate—to start my swing where I thought Trucks was prone to throw it—about crotch high, and up, and if I got started somewhere in between I could adjust in time to get in front of the ball. Otherwise, being as fast as he was, I wouldn't have been able to pull the ball.

One of Mike Epstein's problems when he was with the Senators was in learning to anticipate. He practiced as much and as hard as anybody on our club, but he wasn't practicing the right way. He was having the pitcher in ordinary batting practice tell him what was coming, rather than make a game of it and try to hit anything he saw. I watched him put on a helluva exhibition one day, slamming balls up in the seats, really crashing them, but he called for every pitch.

I didn't say anything then, but the next day I said, "You know, Mike, I could go out there right now as old as I am and do the same thing you did if I know what's coming. What you did was worthless, and it gets you into bad habits besides. Don't tell the pitcher what to throw, learn to hit anything you see." I think it helped him because he had better results after that.

If you're having a problem with a particular pitch, say a slider, a way to solve it is to always anticipate a slider. The last twelve years of my career I looked for the slider almost every pitch because I felt I could do that and still take care of the other pitches. Way back in the 1930s Mel Ott was quoted as saying he always looked for breaking stuff. That's more extreme than looking for a slider because the slider is a much faster pitch than the curve, but Ott felt he got so much breaking stuff it wasn't logical to look for a fastball. Most of the time your strength will take care of itself. If, for example, you're weak on low balls and you anticipate a low ball and here comes a high ball, your strength in that area will take care of itself. The slider is the in-between pitch, and I felt I could adjust to the others. There were times, of course, when I would definitely look for something else, but as a rule I could work off the slider.

Most pitchers are hardheaded enough not to realize you have figured them out. Dick Donovan of the White Sox was a good pitcher and should have been one of the best. He had an exceptionally good slider. He got everybody out on it, but he threw it too often, and for six or seven years I laid for that one pitch and hit a tune on it. Then one day he threw me a big, slow-breaking curve and I looked so bad on it it must have woke him up, because after that he threw me more curves and became a tougher pitcher for me.

Ned Garver was another one. Sliders all the time, and you could anticipate when and where they'd be, usually inside. A guy who can swing a bat is going to hurt a pitcher who throws him inside—from the middle of the plate in. In a jam, I could always figure on a slider from Garver. I got to Garver pretty good.

Then you take pitchers like Whitey Ford or Early Wynn or Ed Lopat or Ted Lyons—moving the ball all the time, giving you something here, then a curve there, then a little extra on the fastball, moving the ball all the time. Much tougher to guess with. A guy like Lyons would fool you because you'd have him figured and he'd come right back and cross you up. Ninth inning, wind blowing out, you have just hit his fastball the last time up, you *know* he can't throw a fastball now, and sure enough he'd throw it and then come right back and throw it again. Lyons was that exception they told me about when I first came up: Don't guess with this guy. Hit what you see. It was fun for a young hitter to face a guy like Lyons. I often wish I could do it all over again.

Now, with a smart pitcher like that, your thinking can change from at bat to at bat. Here's how it might go:

First time up, out on a fastball. Looking for the fastball on the next time up. But you go out on a curve. Third time up, seventh inning, you say to yourself, "Well, he knows I'm a good fastball hitter, and he got me out on a curve. I'm going to look for the curve, even though he got me out on a fastball first time up."

So I take a pitch, a fastball, and it's a strike. Now I *know* I'm going to be looking for the curve. He may be a little extra smart, like Lyons, and thinking, "Well, he's waiting for the curve, I'm still not going to throw it." Sure enough, I take another fastball strike.

I now have to concede to him—because it's two strikes—but I'll be thinking curveball, and if he gets me out all I'll be looking for in the ninth inning is that curve.

Now if he throws a fastball and misses, and throws a curve and misses, and I've got him 2–0, it's pretty academic to look for the fastball on the third pitch. It's the easier pitch for him to get over. If he throws the curve and gets it over, I say to myself, "Well, he's got confidence in it, I'll look for another curve." He threw a curve at 2–0, why wouldn't he throw it again at 2–1? If he then comes back with a fastball at 2–1, playing the game with me, then he's another Ted Lyons and I'm in trouble.

Most pitchers, of course, will have a high enough regard for their repertoire that if they get you out on a good pitch, they'll invariably come back with it. The results of anticipating that pitch have been gratifying to me a thousand times, but I suppose the one I remember best was in the 1941 All-Star game. Two outs, two men on, and the American League trailing 5–4 in the ninth inning.

Claude Passeau of the Cubs was pitching for the National League. Passeau was a good pitcher. He had struck me out in the eighth inning on a fast tailing ball that acted like a slider (they didn't call them sliders in those days). He would jam a left-hander with it and get it past you if you weren't quick. I was late on that one, and as I came up in the ninth I said to myself, "You've got to be quicker, you've got to get more in front." On a 2–1 pitch, he came in with that sliding fastball I was anticipating, and I hit it off the facing of the third deck in right field.

TO THE DRAWING BOARD

All right, so you've done your homework and your thinking is straight. Now the mechanics. Feet and hand position vary more than anything else from player to player because, unlike golf, the baseball swing is not a grooved swing. It is more tailored to the individual, more natural. "Be natural," Tris Speaker used to say, "it's the most important thing."

To hit the ball to the best advantage, I recommend an extremely firm grip, the pressure applied by the fingers and not *against the palms*. The bottom hand holds the bat as you would a hammer or a golf club, the index finger slightly open. Harry Walker was a good student of hitting and he figured the hands should be between 3 to 8 inches from the body, and I'll buy that. But any further emphasis on hand position is not necessary. Where you hold them vertically will vary with the individual. Waiting on the pitch, my hands were just a little below shoulder level. Mel Ott's were way down low, almost at the belt. Earl Averill's were low.

You can adjust to fit your needs. If you want to hit high balls better, if you're having trouble with them, you can raise your hands so that you will be a little quicker getting on top of the ball. But the hands are very much a matter of feel. Give five farm boys five axes and you'll probably get five different hand positions. As long as the position allows you to hit naturally anything within the strike zone, you're all right.

Your weight should be balanced, distributed evenly on both feet and slightly forward on the balls of the feet, with the knees bent and flexible. If you insist on resting back on your heels, find another occupation. The feet are good and planted, the lead foot open so as not to restrict your pivot but slightly closer to the plate than the back foot. I helped brace myself a little by digging a slightly-angled mound for my back foot.

My front foot was on a line with and 12 inches away from the front part of the plate. Rogers Hornsby and Stan Musial stayed deep in the box. Ernie Banks placed his rear foot flush against the back line. Players in the National League for years have tended to stay farther back in the box than American Leaguers, and on the whole their batting averages have been higher. Of course, there is no advantage whatever in being way up front, with your lead foot ahead of the plate, because you are shortening the distance to the pitcher and cheating yourself.

Normally, my feet at the stance were spread 27 inches apart, about average for my size—not nearly as far apart as Joe DiMaggio, who had the widest stance of the great hitters I saw, but much farther apart than Stan Musial, who kept his feet close together and coiled himself at the rear of the batter's box.

Again, this depends on an individual's taste, his size, his bat length, his style. Some of the best hitters did not have classic stances. Lou Boudreau was almost in a sitting position, bent over as he was, and he would straighten up as the ball was thrown. The important thing is to have plate coverage with the bat.

Shoulders should at least start at level; the head is *always* still. Much as in golf, the head stays put, as level as possible, except as you stride into the ball.

I will agree to dropping the head down some to get to a lower pitch, but *do not lunge forward* toward the pitcher, because then you're committing your weight, and the longer you keep from committing yourself, the better your chance of not getting fooled. You fight against going forward, against lunging. Everybody lunges a little—you have to in order to keep your weight balanced as you stride. You can't keep your head perfectly still, as the golfer is told to do, because your lead foot is moving and the head and body come with it to maintain balance. But if you lunge too much, if you come forward too far with your head as you swing, you are diminishing your power. You are escorting the bat instead of swinging it.

Shoulder positions vary. Some batters naturally fall into a low-ball position—that is, with the lead shoulder dropped a little from level. This results in a longer loop in your swing, which you can have on a low ball, where you don't have to be as fast with the bat. The high ball is closer to your hands, and you have to be quicker.

I believe in a *compact stance,* which may come as a surprise. Baseball people used to say, "Keep the arms away from the body, keep 'em

away" (George Sisler said "*Far* away"), but I believe you feel more comfortable and can be quicker with your hands nearer the body—that is, 3 to 8 inches. It's a stronger position. The bat is easier to control when you decrease the arc of the swing.

I held my bat upright, almost perpendicular to the ground. The bat felt lighter that way, more comfortable. It *is* lighter to the holder because as the angle increases, the resistance increases. Hank Greenberg tended to flatten out (his bat more parallel to the ground), but when he started to swing, he cocked it back up a little. Joe DiMaggio held his at about a 45-degree angle and kept it there. So this varies, too.

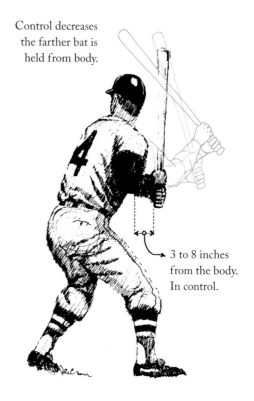

Control decreases the farther bat is held from body.

3 to 8 inches from the body. In control.

My feeling was if I stayed more vertical, thereby increasing the loop in the swing, I could get the ball in the air better, which is advantageous to a power hitter—and no advantage at all to a guy who can't put it in the seats. When I wasn't going well, hitting *too* much into the air, I would start thinking in terms of raising my sights a little, of getting on top of the ball, shortening the swing, and at those times I'd level out the bat a little.

As a left-hand batter, I kept my left elbow straight back, the upper arm perpendicular to the body. I felt it gave me that umph, that little extra something to get the bat moving. This also helped create a wider loop to the swing, the opposite of a chop.

Don't worry if you hitch a little. Everybody says it's awful, but York hitched, Foxx hitched, Greenberg hitched. I dropped down a little, as a cocking action, but the important thing is not to drop your hands too much, because you'll have to bring them back up and that costs time and can disturb your rhythm.

Altogether, much of what you've done up to now has been a matter of personal preference, fitting your individual style and stance to fundamentals, of feeling comfortable and ready in the batter's box. But *everything* you've done is important to you as a hitter, so be alert. After a while you'll see things you never saw before. Even with the batter's box itself.

Fans think they're all alike, and most batters probably do. They're all 4 feet by 6, and they look alike. But it isn't so. I know for a fact the batter's box in Boston was a fraction higher in the back than in the front. I always felt I had a better hold with my back foot when I swung there. In Kansas City, I felt the box slanted the other way—I felt as if I were hitting uphill. I told the groundskeeper about it, and the next time we came into Kansas City it was level. I hit two home runs that day, and when the Kansas City manager learned what had happened he almost fired the groundskeeper.

My first rule of hitting was to get a good ball to hit. I learned down to percentage points where those good balls were. The box shows my particular preferences, from what I considered my "happy zone"—where I could hit .400 or better—to the low outside corner—where the most I could hope to bat was .230. Only when the situation demands it should a hitter go for the low-percentage pitch. Since some players are better high-ball hitters than low-ball hitters, or better outside than in; each batter should work out his own set of percentages. But more important, each should learn the strike zone, because once pitchers find a batter is going to swing at bad pitches he will get nothing else. The strike zone is approximately seven balls wide (allowing for pitches on the corners). When a batter starts swinging at pitches just 2 inches out of that zone (shaded area), he has increased the pitcher's target from approximately 4.2 square feet to about 5.8 square feet—an increase of 37 percent. Allow a pitcher that much of an advantage and you will be a .250 hitter.

.300	.320	.320	.330	.330	.315	.310
.310	.340	.340	.350	.340	.340	.320
.310	.340	.340	.350	.340	.340	.320
.340	.380	.380	.400	.390	.390	.320
.360	.390	.390	.400	.390	.390	.320
.360	.390	.390	.400	.380	.380	.310
.320	.340	.340	.330	.300	.300	.280
.320	.340	.340	.330	.275	.270	.260
.280	.300	.300	.300	.260	.250	.250
.270	.290	.300	.300	.250	.240	.240
.250	.270	.270	.260	.240	.240	.230

From the moment the ball leaves the pitcher's hand, a batter has about two-fifths of a second to make up his mind whether to swing at the pitch and, if he does, to complete his swing. Quickness with the bat is critical. The stance is compact, the lead foot nearer the plate and pointed slightly toward the pitcher, the bat held almost perpendicular to the ground and close to the body. The pitch is on its way. . . .

The lead foot strides 8 inches toward the pitch.

Bat is flattening out, left elbow comes in.

One-second watch times pitch traveling 60′ 6″ to plate at better than 90 mph.

Hips wide open, a line drive is the result.

Wrists are still unbroken through ideal hitting zone.

Hands are already past the plate, well in front.

Hips (*red line*) begin to open up into the pitch.

Bat is flatter still as hips lead way into swing.

A decision is made on the pitch: swing.

Hip action is far ahead, pulling arms around.

Shoulders (*blue line*) begin to open, head is back.

Bat begins a tight but powerful arc into pitch.

Cocking hips (*large arrow*), so essential to the golf swing but never articulated in baseball, is at the root of batting power. It occurs in unison with the beginning of the stride, the lead knee (*arrow*) turning in to facilitate rotation of the hips and shoulders. Note that hands are also cocked.

In fully extended power swing, hands (*arrow*) move

the bat through hitting area as the hips are opened up.

Hands still lead, arms extend, thus increasing arc

of swing to bring fat part of bat up into pitch.

The longer a batter can wait on a pitch, the less chance there is that he will be fooled. But waiting requires quickness. The ball seems on the verge of passing the bat but does not get by.

From the stance to the completion of the swing, hands and forearms supply direction. The grip is firm, with the bottom hand holding the bat like a hammer and the index finger slightly open. Trailing elbows tuck in for compactness, keeping the arc of the swing tight. The wrists do not roll. Action at point of impact is comparable to that of the hard, unbroken swing of an ax.

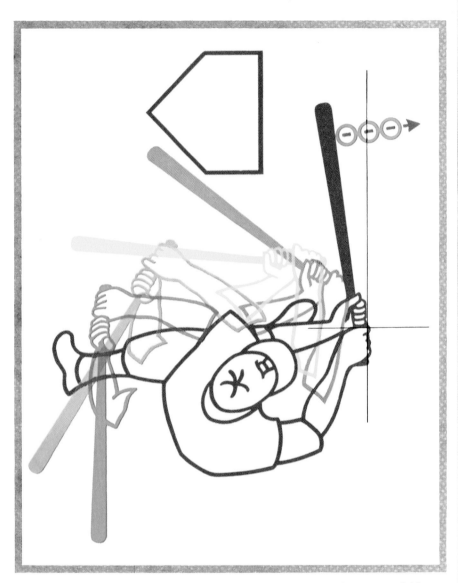

The inside-out swing is a panacea for pull hitters who want to go to the opposite field, even on inside pitches. It is also a remedy for big swingers who strike out often and the ideal protective swing on a two-strike pitch. In executing this push-style swing, batter should try to get on top of ball. Arms are never fully extended, contact is made ideally at 90-degree angle from the direction of pitch, although angles of 15 degrees off optimum are permissible. Hands usually stay ahead; after impact, wrists are still unbroken.

HIPS:
WHERE THE ACTION IS

Now we go into the area that breeds controversy—the moves of the hitter. Many of them have been misunderstood for years, and some of them have been completely overlooked. The most important I can think of is the *cocking* of the *hips*. Sam Snead was once quoted as telling President Eisenhower; "You can't hit with authority until you get your butt into the ball." The advice applies to the baseball hitter.

I was always known as a "wrist" hitter, which was a gross exaggeration, and I'll get to that. But hip cocking is as important as wrist action any day. The way you bring your hips into the swing is directly proportionate to the power you generate. I never saw a good hitter that didn't have good hip cock. With some it was more apparent than others. Joe DiMaggio had it, but it wasn't as noticeable because of his wider stance. All the big home-run hitters had it.

You would think it would be an instinctive thing, something you would pick up in the Little Leagues. Certainly nobody ever had to tell me about it. But I look around at the young hitters today, and 25 percent of them don't cock their hips or hands, don't get themselves ready to hit. Without hip action, you're strictly an arms and wrists hitter.

Now, with your weight evenly distributed, your hips start out at level. You don't worry about hips until you actually begin the performance of the swing. The hips and hands cock as you move your lead foot to stride, the front knee turning in to help the hips rotate back. You are *cocking your hips as you stride*, and it's so important to get that right.

It's a pendulum action. A metronome—move and countermove. You might not have realized it, but you throw a ball that way, you swing a golf club that way, you cast a fishing rod that way. You go back, and then you come forward. You don't start back there. And you don't "start" your swing with your hips cocked.

Ken Harrelson of the Indians was doing that one year. He was concentrating so much on cocking the hips that he was actually doing it at the stance. He had his knee turned in and his hips cocked before the pitch, and without that pendulum action he wasn't generating any power. I made a mistake. I told him about it.

We had a series in Cleveland, and when it was over I had a mutual friend tell Harrelson what he was doing. It was a mistake because I'd forgotten the Indians were coming to Washington the next week. When they got there, Harrelson wasn't cocking prematurely anymore. He beat us twice with home runs. I didn't mind passing on tips like that to opposing players when I was a player myself. After that, I learned to keep my mouth shut.

Your stride is pretty much square to the

Going for power, weight is distributed evenly as bat enters hitting zone. Ideally, it is 15 degrees on either side of perpendicular to pitch, but on sure pull hits up to 30 degrees ahead.

pitcher. It varies in length with the individual. Mine was about 12 inches as a kid, but shortened as the years went by because as I got stronger and quicker I felt it an advantage to stay more within myself, more compact. Be careful not to overstride, because then you spread your hips and prevent a good pivot, diminishing power. The hip movement is a spinning action, with the head as the axis, and it must not be restricted.

The direction of the stride should not vary more than 10 degrees from a perpendicular line toward the pitcher. I saw all the good hitters for the past thirty years, and 90 percent of them strode straight into the ball—Greenberg, DiMaggio, Gehringer, Musial, Kiner, Killebrew. They didn't vary more than 10 degrees from that perpendicular line. They didn't open up more than 10 degrees. Rogers Hornsby stepped in toward the ball a little, and Al Simmons stepped away—he bailed out a little—but both had their weight forward on their feet, both had quick, strong hands and wrists, both got great results.

Mel Ott really bailed out—pulled his foot away from the line, into the bucket—but remember he was hitting in a park made to order for pull hitting, the old Polo Grounds in New York, where it was 290 feet down the line. Vern Stephens was a hell of a hitter, and he opened up as he strode, but these are exceptions. An exceptionally strong guy can get away with things. Too, Mel Ott stood so close to the plate that when he did bail out he still had plate coverage with the bat.

Ty Cobb and some others used to say the direction of the stride depended on where the pitch was—inside pitch, you'd bail out a little; outside, you'd move in toward the plate. This is wrong because it's impossible. It is only 60.5 feet from pitcher to batter. If the pitcher throws the ball 90 miles per hour, it takes less than 0.40 second for the ball to reach the batter, even without allowing for the 4 or 5 feet a pitcher comes down the mound before releasing the ball. (That's what you're working with: 0.40 second, with a round ball and a round bat—and you still don't think it's the toughest thing to do in sport?)

Actually, you the batter have already made your stride before you know where the ball will be or what it will be (a batter can't recognize the pitch much before it has come a third

of the way, which cuts his reaction time even further); you have made it in that split second the pitcher's arm comes into that little area over his shoulder you're focusing on (think of it as a 15-inch square—the ball comes out there).

You have cocked and made your stride— but *you have not moved your head* more than that little bit required to keep proper balance. You haven't shifted your weight from one foot to the other, but have maintained balance, the weight evenly distributed, the hands back, the bat cocked.

FIRST UP IS KEY UP

All right. Stop and think. This is your first time up in a game. You are not concerned about mechanics now. Your practice time has made them automatic. Nervous? Nothing wrong with that. I think it's good to be a little nervous. My impression when I first saw Carl Yastrzemski was, "Gee, what a twitchy guy this is, all coiled up like a spring, ready to pop, just can't wait to hit." Naturally, if you're so nervous it affects your control at the plate, then you've got a problem, but that won't happen very often if you've got your mind on the business at hand, which is:

You are thinking strictly about getting a good ball to hit, and remembering what to expect from the pitcher.

For me as a batter hitting third in the lineup, there was one thing that was 95 percent certain: I was going to *take the first pitch*. Even a strike right down the middle. The reason I swung on the other 5 percent was that occasionally I got one that was so tempting, such a big balloon coming in, that I took a cut to keep the pitcher honest.

But what advantage is there in taking the first pitch in a game (the rule doesn't apply in succeeding times up) if the pitch is a strike and you've automatically reduced by 33 percent the number of strikes you'll get? These advantages: You've refreshed your memory of the pitcher's speed and his delivery. You see if he's got it on this particular day. You've given yourself a little time to get settled, to get the tempo.

I guarantee this: If you held a $50,000 home-run contest for Ruth and Mantle and DiMaggio and Hornsby and Foxx and anybody else, giving each one six *swings,* every one of them would take a couple pitches before they swung. Just for fun, see what first-ball hitters average the next time you go to the park or watch a game on television. I'll bet there won't be one hit in ten, or even two solidly hit outs.

Sure, the tendency might have been to groove the first pitch on me, but I still didn't feel my chances were good because I hadn't seen a pitch. Make a mistake—swing late on a fastball, pop up—and you're out, and the next time up there might be a couple men on base in a tight spot and you're still not sure what to expect.

And despite taking that first pitch, I was still pitched to carefully—an indication of respect, I guess, or maybe that the pitchers didn't trust me. (I hit a home run off Bob Lemon on a first pitch one time, and he yelled, "What the hell are you doing?" He was one guy I didn't want to get ahead of me.) Usually I'd get to see four or five pitches that first time up, maybe even six, and I was learning on them all the time. Second time up, you're even *more* alert, because now you've had a sampling: What did I do the first time? A home run off what pitch? A groundout? A strikeout? Why? Did he fool me?

There is much more to that first time up than just taking a pitch, there is the continuing matter of proper thinking, and I want to elaborate on it here where it is so important. Nobody has ever said this around me, or, as far as I know, even thought it—but the first time at bat has to be a key to effective hitting, a key to the day you are going to have and therefore a key to your baseball life because the days pile one on another to make a career. You must learn to *make* that first time up a key time by striving to find out as much about a pitcher as possible, and you do that by *making him pitch*.

It's simple arithmetic: You figure to face a pitcher at least three or four times in a game. The more information you log the first time up, the better your chances the next three. The more you make him pitch, the more information you get.

What do you learn first time up? You will probably see the pitcher at his best. You will see what his ball is doing, what kind of breaking stuff he has, what kind of pattern he is working out for you. For example, say the first time up with the count 2–1 you see a curve and, bang, you hit it. Now, *he* will remember you hit it, if he's any kind of a pitcher. But if he's essentially a curveball pitcher—you will have found this out in previous games—you might calculate he will come back with the curve again. If you've been alert you have stored away some tendencies—the pitches he got you out on, the circumstances of the game, the last game, the last year: How did he pitch to you? You might have hit a fastball. What was the count? What was the situation? Was it a good pitch? Did the pitcher put it where he wanted it? How good did you hit it? Is this going to scare him the rest of the day?

Past confrontations should be going through your mind, but more important than anything else that first time up—and this applies whether you've hit against him in the past or not—is *you want to make him pitch*.

And the first rule of thumb is this:

Don't hit at anything you haven't seen.

When I played, I batted third in the lineup. I'd watch the pitcher warm up, but you can't see all you want to see from that distance because it's never the same as being in the batter's box facing him. The lead-off man has a little advantage because he can stand up there pretty close during the warm-up. (Sometimes when I led off an inning later in the game I'd get so close watching a pitcher that guys like Frank Lary would brush me back a little, letting me know they didn't appreciate that close a scrutiny. I liked to look them over.) The thing is, no matter who the pitcher is—a Feller or a Grove or a Ford or whoever—his stuff is better some days than others. One day he will have that little extra zip, that little extra umph on his fastball or curve.

So you haven't seen it and you have to know: Is it that little extra today or isn't it? Nobody has good enough timing or good enough vision to get up there cold and determine that difference right away. But if you take a couple of pitches, your chances are better. Now, the crux of the matter: Hitting is 50 percent from the neck up. You are not just taking pitches, you are taking specific pitches. You learn from them.

I said I took the first pitch almost every time I batted the last ten or twelve years I played. Every pitcher knew it, and they *all* tried to lay one in there. When they missed (threw a ball instead of a strike), I didn't necessarily take the next one. I didn't necessarily take a strike because I wasn't just taking a strike by taking that first pitch the way people might have thought. I had quite another motive:

I didn't want to hit until I had seen a fastball.

Why? Because the fastball clears you up for everything. If it has that little extra something on that particular day when the pitcher is at his best, then you're that much surer of getting the tempo, or knowing how long you can wait. If the first pitch was a curve and a strike, then I didn't feel I had the same advantage, but in my case—always taking the first pitch—I was too great a temptation. The pitcher laid in a fastball 99 percent of the time.

Now, once you've seen the fastball, there's nothing else to look for for the time being. (Don't hit at anything you haven't seen, remember?) If you're looking for the fastball and he throws a curve, so much the better: you've learned a little more. You know his fastball is *x* fast, and you're geared for it, and now you've seen his curve. If the curve fools you—that's important: *If* it fools you—or if it's in a tough spot, chances are you will take that, too, that first time up. If you weren't fooled, and saw it coming, with one strike you might go ahead and swing, but appraise it nevertheless: Was it good? How much did it fool you? How big did you see it?

If it really fooled you, take stock: "Boy, this guy's pretty tough. I've got to lay back a little." And now with two strikes you will have to resort to techniques we will elaborate on later—ways of conceding to the pitcher.

We have already discounted the first pitch as a pitch worth swinging at. Your chances of hitting a first pitch are never very good: it may be a curve that fools you, or a fastball that has that little extra, or maybe a new pitch the pitcher is trying. And applying the above rule of thumb (don't hit at anything you haven't seen), you will probably look at a couple more before you begin to appreciate the pitcher's repertoire and what you must do to handle him. Making him pitch, however, has allowed you to gear up, to get the tempo, and maybe if you're alert enough the results will be immediate. Nothing pleased me more when I played than to work a pitcher to 2–2 or 3–2, maybe foul a couple off, and then walk or get a base hit. Then I knew I really had something going for the day.

There is one very important side effect—a team effect, actually—of an individual exercising this kind of discipline his first time up, and the point seems to be lost on so many people in baseball. If you've made that pitcher pitch, if you've made him throw four or five or maybe six or seven times, right away, and if the batter behind you does the same thing, and all nine guys in the lineup do it, the pitcher will have pitched the equivalent of *half a game in three or four innings*. The effect should be telling: He will probably be out of

Hip action: unrestricted (*above*) leads power thrust of swing; restricted (*right*) eliminates power entirely.

there, worn out, by the sixth or seventh inning. Compound the situation and say it's a real hot day, and he's a little wild and he walks a couple guys. He could be on the ropes even sooner.

But how often do you see it happen? A guy starts off wild, throws a couple in the dirt, then the batter swings at the first strike and pops up. Then the next guy does the same thing: two or three bad pitches, and then a groundout, then a couple more bad pitches, and the batter swings at the nearest pitch available and fouls out. Instead of wearing him out, you've helped him out. A pitcher is lucky to face such dumb hitters. Too many hitters boot the ball in just this manner: *They don't make the pitcher pitch.*

I've heard batters try to argue the point. They say, "Well, I can't do that, I can't be that selective because I miss too many balls." A perfect example is Frank Howard. Frank says he can't hit well with two strikes because he misses too many. Well, the ones he is missing are the ones in a tough spot or the ones he has been fooled on and shouldn't even try to hit before two strikes anyway.

The fact is that when Howard gets his pitch he does just about as good a job on it as anybody in the American League—*when he gets his pitch*. He might not be able to handle as big an area as, say, Frank Robinson, but in his area he is as good as anybody. The best hitters can take care of the whole strike zone, but then all have certain spots they hit better in. If you start going out of your area, you're

just helping the pitcher. The very best pitchers would have a hard time throwing the ball consistently in a foot square. That's about their limit. You make them work, make them throw curves, fastballs, sliders, and they will eventually miss and give you the opening you want.

So: Make the pitcher pitch.

HIPS LEAD THE WAY

The next pitch is on its way, and your hips and hands are cocked, your head staying back in place, your whole body more or less coiled for the opposite and equal application of power—the swivel or pivot, the opening of the hips. As the hips come around, the hands follow, just as in golf, and the bat follows the hands, and as they get into the hitting area the speed is increasing. One naturally follows the other. You can't get the proper action without the hips clearing the way. (Try it for yourself: have a teammate stand behind you and hold you by the sides of your pants, just below the waist. Try to swing. All arms and wrists, and no power.)

The pitch is in your happy zone, and you're after it, intent on getting that 4 ½-inch joy part of the bat—the real fat of the bat (see diagram)—on the ball coming toward you at 90 miles an hour. At this point you're trying to be as quick as possible with your bat without losing control. I would guess your shoulders and hip turn are operating at 80 to 85 percent capacity. Any more than that and you lose control and could overswing, the timing goes, the balance goes. I always liked to feel I had

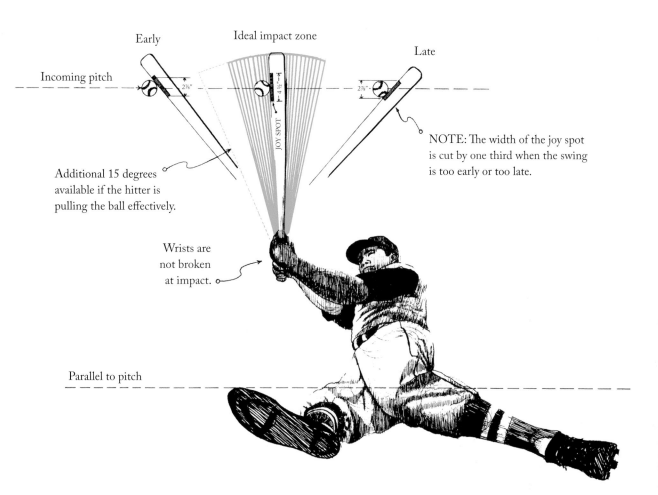

Early

Ideal impact zone

Late

Incoming pitch

2⅞"

2⅞"

JOY SPOT

NOTE: The width of the joy spot is cut by one third when the swing is too early or too late.

Additional 15 degrees available if the hitter is pulling the ball effectively.

Wrists are not broken at impact.

Parallel to pitch

a little something extra left in my shoulders and hips, to maintain control. But *not in my hands, arms and wrists*. With them it was 100 percent.

Now, two points of major importance, and you will be surprised hearing them from a "wrist" hitter and a "pull" hitter. No doubt I was a pull hitter, and no doubt the ideal hit is a pulled ball 380 feet because that's a home run in most parks in the big leagues.

At advantageous moments, when the count is right—3 and 0, 3 and 1, 2 and 0—and the pitcher has got to get it over, or it's a time in the game when a long hit is absolutely essential, the pulled line drive is worth shooting for.

But take a look at the diagram above. The best chance of getting the joy spot of your bat on the ball occurs when the swing brings it into contact at 90 degrees from the direction of the pitch. At that point, the joy spot is fully exposed—4 ½ inches. The more you sharpen the angle of the bat, the more you diminish your good hitting surface.

Fifteen degrees either side of 90 degrees from the direction of the pitch is a reasonable tolerance area. An extra 15 degrees in front is available for a batter pulling the ball well. But at 45 degrees—the real pull swing—you've cut the joy spot one third. If you are that far ahead of the ball, you also reduce the time you have to judge the pitch, and as I said there is no greater luxury than time because the longer you can wait the less chance you will be fooled.

I hated to be early on a pitch because everything is wrong then—I wasn't waiting, I was probably fooled, I was too far in front to hit the ball with authority. If I was behind a little, it didn't hurt as much because if you are quick with the bat—and I preach quickness—you'll do all right. Hit in back of that 15 degrees from perpendicular, however, and you probably will not have enough bat speed or length of stroke built up to hit with authority.

When I had such a hard time with Boudreau's shift, and ones like it that sprung up in 1947 and afterward, I survived by learning to hit to left field. Everybody was saying—and

Both the bat and the ball have joy spots.

the Boston writers were writing—that I wasn't trying to hit to left, that I was too stubborn, that all I cared about was ramming the ball into the teeth of that shift, getting base hits in spite of it. The fact was, I was having a hard time learning to hit to left. It wasn't because I didn't get any advice. Of that I got a truckload.

Ty Cobb wrote me a two-page letter, outlining how he would do it. We met at Yankee Stadium during the 1947 World Series, and he took me around behind a telephone booth and we talked. He said, "Oh, boy, Ted, if they had ever pulled that stuff on me, that drastic shift . . . ," and his mouth was watering, seeing in his mind's eye the immortal Ty Cobb lashing the ball into that open range in left field.

Well, Cobb was more of a push hitter, a slap hitter. He choked up 2 inches from the bottom and held the bat with his hands 4 inches apart. He stood close to the plate, his

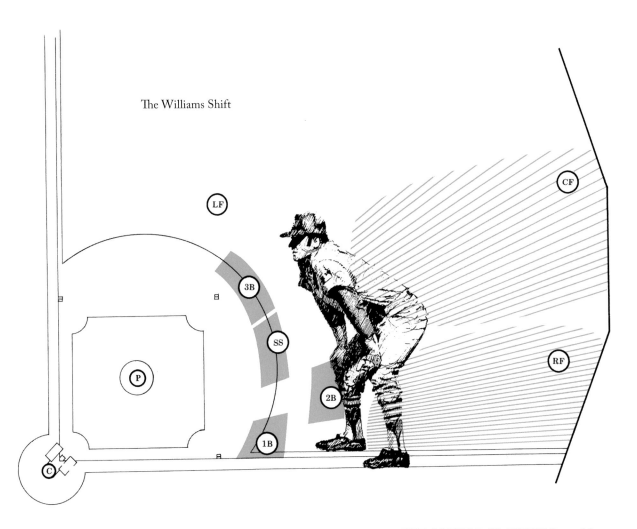

The Williams Shift

hands forward. He had great ability to push the ball, to lash hits all around. He was a great athlete, maybe the greatest, but he was a completely different animal from me, and his words were like Greek.

The arc of my swing was much greater than Cobb's. What he said would apply to guys more his type, guys who choked up on the bat more and pushed the ball around. That wasn't in me. I was down, with a longer stroke, a greater arc.

When I beat the shift, I did it by taking my stance a little farther from the plate, striding slightly more into the pitch—but concentrating on getting on top of the ball and pushing it. A *push* swing, an inside-out swing, fully extended, the *hands ahead of the fat part of the bat*. This produced contact at 90 degrees or more from the direction of the pitch, and sent

the ball to the left of the pitcher's box, away from the shift. Almost like hitting pepper. Pepper can help you with this technique. In fact, pepper is a great warm-up game for any hitter, and as a manager I'm going to insist that the Senators do more of it. I was always amazed when I'd go to the Red Sox camp those last years to see them playing *volley*ball, when pepper is ten times better exercise for ballplayers—pitchers included.

During those experiments, I also learned another thing that most young hitters and 50 percent of the big-league players I've talked to have never considered—that the impact of bat on ball is reached *not* with the wrists rolling, or a "wrist" swing, but with the wrists square and *unbroken*, as they would be at impact when an ax is swung on a tree. The power is always applied *before the wrists roll*. Even when you are pulling? Yes, because the hips bring the bat around, not the wrists.

Try it for yourself. Get a bat and swing it against a telephone pole. I do this with doubting young Washington players. Where is the wrist position at point of impact? Square and unbroken, that's where, just as when you hit a tree with an ax. Conclusion? *The baseball swing is a hard push swing.* You are pushing right through the impact area, about 6 to 8 inches on a plane with the flight of the ball. You get your power not so much from the wrists or the arms and shoulders, but from the rotation of the hips into the ball. When you are effectively pulling the ball, you may notice that the top wrist does "break" a little, just at impact,

but it is a very slight break and it is *definitely not a roll.*

This is not to say you need not have strong wrists. You do need them. And strong arms, shoulders, back, and legs. I was always squeezing rubber balls, working hand grips, doing fingertip push-ups, swinging heavy bats, doing chin-ups, running, walking, anything to get stronger. But wrist action is overemphasized.

The wrists roll after the ball has left the bat. The "snap" that everyone (including me) used to say was so important comes after you hit the ball. It occurs only in the follow-through. Obviously you don't follow through with stiff wrists. So many hitters used to say, "No wrist roll, no power." They were wrong.

If you still don't believe it, grab a bat and start into your swing. When you get over the plate before the wrists roll, stop and have another player apply pressure to the end of the bat from the direction of the pitcher. Check the amount of resistance you can give him. Then roll your wrists and let him apply pressure again. If you can resist as well in that position, you are the rare exception. (I don't happen to believe there *is* an exception.) The unbroken wrists is a much stronger position.

One point must be re-emphasized, however: The hips set the swing in motion and lead the way. If they are restricted, if you don't open them wide enough, the wrists will roll prematurely. They won't stay in that good strong position long enough to make proper contact. If contact is made as the wrists roll, chances are, the bat will be on top of the ball and a weak ground ball will result. It is absolutely useless to pull the ball if you do that, of course. If you're going to pull the ball, you ought to be able to get it into the air.

One other thing. I said I moved away to help myself hit the inside pitch to left field. Be careful with this, because if you move too far away from the plate, there's a disadvantage, too: If you're too deep, the balls that break over the front corners of the plate are difficult to reach. And they are still strikes.

A very important adjustment must be made when you move back from the plate (see diagram). To maintain your length of stroke, you must close your stance in proportion to the distance you have moved the back foot away. In other words, to keep everything constant you must rotate the whole stance around, bringing your lead foot *in* as you move your back foot away.

This will give the hitter with problems another big advantage: more time. You are always fighting for more time. Moving away and around in this manner gives you roughly two feet more room in back to wait for the pitch. And, of course, it virtually eliminates the pulled ball. The reverse is obvious: The closer your back foot to the plate, the more you have to open up the lead foot. This gives you less time because you will be hitting the ball farther out front. It will also allow you to pull the ball, and when you are hitting well this is something to strive for. The more you open up, the more you make yourself pull.

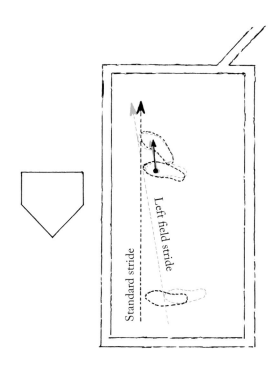

THE POWER HAND— WHICH IS IT?

I said at the beginning that you would be surprised to hear that Ted Williams thinks he might have been a better left-hand hitter if he had not been a natural right-hander. I could rephrase that to say I think I would have been a better hitter if I had also been a left-hand thrower. I was right-handed, and I don't know why but from the time I was old enough to carry a bat to the sandlots of San Diego, I hit lefty.

Of the nine outstanding left-hand hitters in baseball history, Ty Cobb, Joe Jackson, and I were the only three who were natural right-handers. Ruth, Gehrig, Sisler, Terry,

Musial, and Speaker were lefties all the way—throwing and batting left-handed. To my knowledge, there was never a great natural left-hander who batted right-handed.

What am I driving at? Just this: Ideally, for maximum power and efficiency, you want your stronger hand closer to the point of impact. If you're a natural right-hander batting left-handed as I did, your strong hand—the right—is *not* closer to the impact.

The same thing applies in golf. For years they tried to make people believe that a right-hand swinger got his power from the left hand. Baloney. They were saying, in effect, that it was a right-hand game played left-handed, and Snead and Palmer came out and said that was baloney, too. Lately they've been admitting it: If you're right-handed, your chief power source is your right hand, the hand nearer the club head. Tommy Armour was saying it long before the others. He had it in a book, *How to Play Your Best Golf All the Time*, under a no-nonsense piece of instruction that read: "Whack the hell out of the ball with your right hand!"

What about switch-hitters? Hank Aaron was quoted as saying some years ago that he wished he had been a switch-hitter. I wouldn't

THE SLIGHT UPSWING IS BEST*

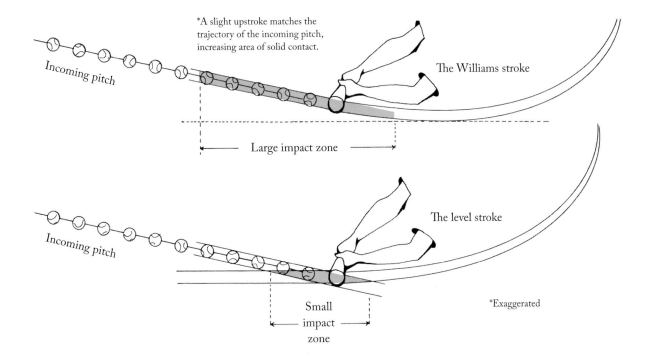

*A slight upstroke matches the trajectory of the incoming pitch, increasing area of solid contact.

Incoming pitch

The Williams stroke

Large impact zone

Incoming pitch

The level stroke

Small impact zone

*Exaggerated

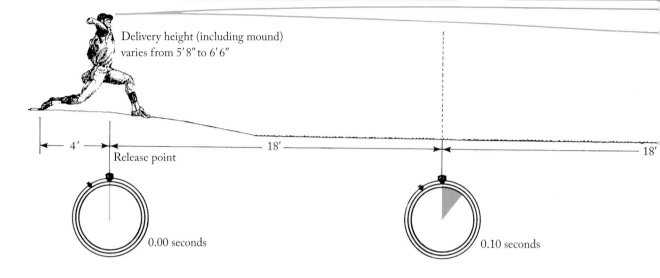

Delivery height (including mound) varies from 5′8″ to 6′6″

4′

Release point

18′

18′

0.00 seconds

0.10 seconds

discourage it as a manager if a guy thinks he can do it, if he has inclinations that way, and if he is truly ambidextrous enough to be effective at it. Give it a chance at a young age if you feel you must. Experiment. But for me and for most hitters, I'd say no. The switch-hitter is usually stronger one way than the other, and invariably the strong side is where his strong hand is on top, nearer the point of impact. Reggie Smith of the Red Sox, for example, hit the ball harder right-handed, he had a quicker bat right-handed—and he was a natural right-hander.

I think anybody would agree that Mickey Mantle, maybe the greatest power switch-hitter of all time, was a better right-hand hitter. He was a natural right-hander. He had to be quicker, stronger, better when he swung

that way because his power hand was closer to the head of the bat.

Batting left-handed, he had the advantage of a short right-field fence in Yankee Stadium and with his speed he was an excellent bunter left-handed. It is also true that he got ample opportunities to bat right-handed there because, due to the park dimensions, most clubs load up with left-handed pitchers against the Yankees. I thought he might have still batted right-handed against right-handed pitchers in certain parks, like Fenway in Boston, where the fence in left is so short, but he didn't.

When I was helping coach the Red Sox in the spring, I couldn't get anybody to believe that Reggie Smith would wind up being a better right-hand batter. Bobby Doerr disagreed with me; everybody did. Eventually,

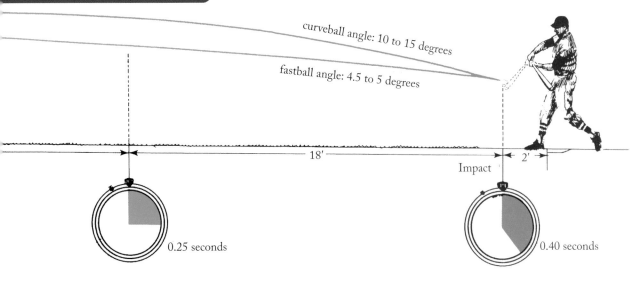

curveball angle: 10 to 15 degrees

fastball angle: 4.5 to 5 degrees

18′

Impact

2′

0.25 seconds

0.40 seconds

I asked Reggie, "Are you a better right-hand hitter or left-hand hitter?"

"Left," he said.

I said, "Someday you're going to be a better right-hand hitter," and he is today. At least in my opinion.

UP, UP IS THE WAY

Now, what about that "level" swing? As I said, you have always heard that the ideal swing is level or "down." Your swing often coincides with your physical capabilities. Certainly a Nellie Fox had more of a level swing than a Mickey Mantle, because Nellie didn't knock down fences. Fox was a great little punch hitter who concentrated on getting a piece of the ball, on being quick with the bat, on directing balls sharply through the holes instead of

up in the air. He had his sights high—to get on top of the ball. A fly ball from a light hitter is usually an out. When the ball is on the ground, it puts a greater burden on the fielders. Things can happen.

But if you get the ball into the air with power, you have the gift to produce the most important hit in baseball—the home run. More important is that you hit consistently with authority. For those purposes, I advocate a slight *up*swing (from level to about 10 degrees), and there is another good reason for this—the biggest reason:

Say the average pitcher is 6 foot 2. He's standing on a mound 10 inches high. He's pitching overhand or three-quarter arm. He releases the ball right about ear level. Your strike zone is, roughly, from 22 inches to 4 feet 8. Most pitchers will come in below the waist, because the low pitch is tougher to hit. The flight of the ball is *down* (see diagram), about 5 degrees. A slight upswing—again, led by the hips coming around and up—puts the bat flush in line with the path of the ball for a longer period—that 12- to 18-inch impact zone.

Ken McMullen, formerly with the Senators, is an example. McMullen had a good year for us after a bad start, and he did it by adjusting from a downswing to an upswing. He did it all himself. All I said was, "Look, Mac, you're swinging down on the ball too much. You're swinging *down*." I got two players, Epstein and another guy, and I said, "Okay, Mac, swing the bat." He swung and I put my bat on the line of his swing and held it there. I said, "Okay, Mike, you swing." We held the other bat on the line of Epstein's swing and put the two lines together.

Now, it's true that Epstein swung up a little too much, but there was too much difference between his and McMullen's, and Mac saw it, too. He was hitting about .235 with eight home runs at the All-Star break. He ended up hitting .272 and nineteen home runs. He began to get that hard overspin on ground balls, and they were going through the infield with something on them. When he hit it solid, boy, it went. He hit the longest ball he ever hit at the stadium, way up in the upper deck.

Revert briefly to what I said about unbroken wrists and the importance of hip action. You can tie the three together right here.

Swing level (or what is commonly called "down"), and the tendency is to bring your top hand over the ball at impact. The effect is a tack-hammer stroke, almost a "roll"—and it is not what you want. You'll find that even without good hip action you can swing in that manner, and the result is a minimum of power.

But if you swing slightly *up* you *have* to have the hips leading and then out of the way, generating speed and power, and you will find your top hand (right hand for right-handed batter, left hand for left-handed batter) is in the strongest possible position: wrist unbroken and directly behind the ball at impact. The result: a ball hit with greater power and authority.

Certainly there are times when you want to think more about getting on top of the ball—times when you are having trouble, getting fooled, popping up. The upswing is harder for one reason: It's a longer stroke with a longer loop to it. It requires more time. When I say "get on top of the ball," I don't mean to swing down or chop, but to get your sights higher and level out your swing more. Nine times out of ten when you fail to make contact with a pitch, you have swung under it.

The level swing—or, when you're really having trouble, the "push" swing—is the shortest possible stroke; you have less chance of hitching, or overswinging. It helps you get back on top of the ball and, more important, gives you more time to wait, to keep from getting fooled. It is also the ideal two-strike swing, and here is where so many of today's

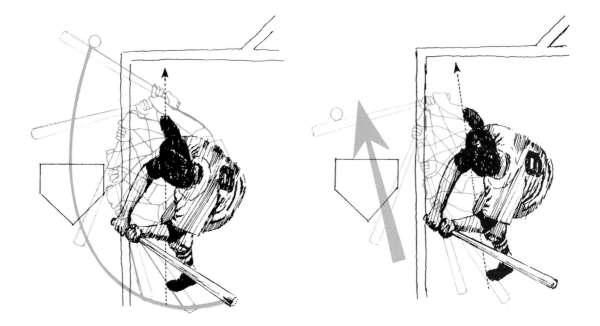

hitters are failing, aren't hitting as many singles and doubles, aren't hitting .300, but are striking out so much. *They don't protect themselves on a two-strike pitch.* Two strikes and they're still swinging 100 percent, trying to pull, trying to hit the ball into the seats.

In my day, the big swingers were Greenberg, Foxx, Kiner, Mize, and Mantle, but they also hit for average. There were others like Gus Zernial, Pat Seerey, and Chet Laabs who were sluggers, too, but who struck out a lot. They were big swingers *all* the time. Instead of outstanding slugger-hitters, they were outstanding sluggers, period. As good as they are, Reggie Jackson and Dave Kingman tend to fall in this category.

All right. What do you do about being the complete hitter? Up to two strikes, you have

been selective. With two strikes, the advantage turns; you now have to concede to the pitcher. You have to make adjustments. You have to think in terms of making everything *quicker*.

How do you do that? You choke up a little bit. You quit trying to pull. You think more about that push swing, that 90-degree impact from the direction of the pitch. You think about hitting the ball back through the box. Harry Walker was a great student of hitting and he was good at this. Joe DiMaggio, Joe Cronin, George Kell, Lou Boudreau, Harvey Kuenn—they could do it. Rod Carew, George Brett, Wade Boggs, Don Mattingly, and Pete Rose are probably the most flexible hitters around today.

When you've shortened up and quickened

up, you can wait longer, you get fooled less, you become more consistent getting good wood on the ball. Psychologically, becoming a good two-strike hitter inspires confidence. A batter knows he can still hit with authority. He learns, as I did, that he can cut strikeouts to less than fifty a year. He can bat 20 or 30 points higher. In 1957, when I hit .388, I got a lot of my big hits on two-strike pitches. In fact, most of my career I was an effective two-strike hitter—not so great a percentage of home runs but a high average of hits on two-strike pitches. Harry Heilmann told me years ago that when he learned the inside-out swing and knew he could hit the inside pitch to right field, he quit worrying about two-strike pitches. Heilmann was one of the greatest right-hand hitters of them all. As a young player with the Red Sox I made it a point to talk hitting with Heilmann whenever we went into Detroit.

CORRECTIONS AND ADJUSTMENTS

The reason hitting a baseball is so tough is that even the best can't hit all the balls just right. To do so is a matter of corrections every minute, in practice as well as in the game.

Ground out a lot? You're probably swinging too early. Popping up? Probably swinging late. It's a slight *up*swing, remember, and when you're late you're under the ball, when you're early you're on top.

The batter who is alert will consider the environment, the park, the background. What kind of a day is it? Is the wind blowing a gale from center field? If so, it will be silly to try to hit the ball 480 feet. Strive to have more finesse that day, to exercise greater bat control, to be more conscious of hitting through the middle, of hitting line drives.

Is it damp and rainy? The ball you hit won't go as far because on a damp day the air is heavier. A curveball pitcher will be even more effective on a heavy day. Be alert to these things.

And what about when you're in a tight spot and a big black cloud suddenly looms up? What do you do if you're up there and it suddenly goes dark?

What I did was yell "time" and step out of the box, put my finger in my eye, and complain about a cinder. Unless you know for a fact that your eyes can dilate quickly enough in that split second to adjust to a light that might be half the candle power, you'd be foolish to stand in there and try to hit. Step out and wait until the cloud passes, or until your eyes have dilated and are accustomed to the new light.

If you're playing in a perpetual bad light— some parks are not lit as well as others, or don't have as good a background—then you might think in terms of conceding to the pitcher, the same as when you have two strikes. Or maybe you're hurt a little, not enough to put you out of the game but an eye that is bothering you or a sprained thumb—again, think in terms of conceding to the pitcher. Choke up. Try hitting through the middle. I remember Al

Rosen of the Indians in an All-Star game one year, playing with a real bad wrist. He couldn't swing as easily, taped up as much as he was, but he choked up more than he ever had, and he hit two home runs that day.

I happen to be a nut about distractions at the plate, but I think a lot of hitters aren't smart enough to realize how much a distraction can be a detriment to good hitting, no matter how small. A white shirt in the center-field bleachers, a house that stands out through the trees, a scoreboard in the line of vision—they can all be distractions. Shadows can disturb a hitter, and if it were up to me, there would be a number of parks in baseball that would be made to turn on the lights whenever those shadows become a factor. In the meantime, the hitter has to adjust whatever way he can.

Much of the correction concerns the

pitchers you face. Against a guy who has you hitting ground balls, you have to think in terms of making him come up with his pitches. If he consistently makes you hit the ball in the air—if, say, his ball is riding—you think in terms of getting on top, of being a little quicker with your swing. High-riding fastball pitchers like Feller and, today, Jim Palmer of Baltimore have to be adjusted to by thinking about swinging down on the ball, though in actuality you aren't swinging down at all, but simply getting more on top. It feels that way because you've started higher and you've shortened your swing to be quicker.

Many times in my career I'd be late—underneath—a high fastball and I'd think to myself, "Be quicker, get on top." I'd psyche myself that way. And, in order to be even quicker, I'd make one other adjustment: I'd flatten out my bat a little at the stance (as opposed to holding it vertical to the ground). This decreases the loop of the swing and allows me to get on top of the ball quicker. Paul Waner used to say you uppercut a low pitch, and that can be effective, but I don't recommend it. I'd say to go down a little, don't stay quite as high, bend your knees down toward the pitch. That way your swing will stay more uniform. The tendency on a low ball is to hit it on the ground. If you bend your knees and go down with the pitch you'll be able to get under it enough to compensate. Don't misunderstand me—I'm not saying you don't swing up on a low ball (again, and if I sound obsessed with the idea, it is because I am; I advocate the up swing). I'm saying that

to get the maximum hitting surface of the bat through the longest possible impact zone you are better off bending your knees and dropping down. The angle of the bat at impact is much sharper when you're up high trying to uppercut. The plane of the swing intersects the downward flight of the ball over a shortened area. You want the opposite.

I suppose I could name a hundred pitchers who were tough for me, all requiring the utmost concentration. Some of the great ones I caught near the end of their careers—Buck Newsom, Mel Harder, Red Ruffing, Tommy Bridges, Ted Lyons, Lefty Gomez.

If you asked me to name the five toughest, you might be surprised at my answer: Whitey Ford, Bob Lemon, Ed Lopat, Bob Feller, and Hoyt Wilhelm. All different from each other, but smart as hell. A second five would be right up there: Paul Trout, Virgil Trucks, Hal Newhouser, Vic Raschi, Allie Reynolds, but they were real power pitchers, guys who stood out there and dared you to hit their best stuff.

As a hitter I could handle the fastball pitchers, at least with more consistency. I hit twelve home runs off Trucks. He was the president of the club. I hit ten off Bob Feller and Ned Garver, eight off Fred Hutchinson, Early Wynn, and Jim Bunning. Among the fastball pitchers, I suppose Joe Page got me out as many times as anybody. When he first came into the league with the Yankees, he had a good, live fastball. He didn't strike me out much, but I had a hard time getting hold of his pitches.

I didn't dread facing any of them, but when I went into a game knowing the pitcher was tough, it was better for me. Invariably, when I'd say, "Boy, I'm going to bust this guy," it wouldn't happen.

The best all had good deliveries. They weren't stereotyped. They never conceded to the hitter. Three-and-one count and they'd still give you tough pitches. Cleveland's Bob Lemon was a great natural athlete; his ball was always moving, always sinking, always in a tough spot. Bob Feller, also of Cleveland, I put in there because he probably had more stuff than anybody, though I hit him pretty well. Even after losing his stuff, he won on control.

Ed Lopat and Whitey Ford of the Yankees were left-handers. Lopat had as fine a collection of junk as you'll ever see. He called

(*Left to right*) Hoyt Wilhelm, Whitey Ford, Ed Lopat, and Bob Lemon

it barnyard stuff. He was always giving you something new. Ford had that sharp-breaking curve, and he always got it in a good spot, away and down. Most of the hits I got off Ford were to center and left center. He made very few mistakes. The only home run I hit off Ford was on a high curve, and that was the only high curve I ever saw from Ford. It was in the seventh or eighth inning, and he was probably tired.

Wilhelm? Pitched until he was forty-nine and made the Hall of Fame—and he was a knuckleballer all the way. What do you do with a knuckleball? The guy that finds out should write his own book about it. Don't ask me, because I seldom hit it, but I'd say you never try to pull it, for one thing. You don't try to get big with it, you just stay with it as long as possible.

Wilhelm was the guy who would throw you a sure-strike knuckler, then a real good knuckler, then with two strikes, an utterly unhittable knuckler, dancing in your face. I always looked for knucklers with Wilhelm. I remember one time, waiting for that knuckler, and darn if he didn't throw a fastball. I said, to myself, "Well, gee, here's a nice fastball," *pow*, line drive into right field for a base hit. I had that much time. He never gave me another.

The bad thing about the knuckleball, of

Bob Feller

course, is that it's not only hard to hit, it's even hard to catch. It can be a liability if you've got a catcher who can't handle it, and most catchers can't. I'd like to know how many times Wilhelm ran into problems because his catchers couldn't hold him. He'd strike guys out and they *still* got on base because the ball went through the catcher. Poor Gus Triandos. He had to wear that big oversized glove, and it got to be a joke in Baltimore the number of passed balls he ran up.

OF PITCHERS AND STUBBORNNESS

The trouble with the average pitcher is his hardheadedness. He has too inflated an opinion of what he's got. Say it's his fastball. He thinks he can throw it anytime, anyplace, anywhere. If you hit his fastball, he still gives it to you again.

John Rigney was like that. He would put it in there, and you would put it out. Robin Roberts stayed with his fastball almost three years after he'd lost it—then he learned to pitch without it. All the great hitters could hit fastballs no matter how fast the pitcher was.

Average pitchers don't spend enough time studying hitters. They concede too often to a hitter in a tough spot. Their biggest mistake is they don't work on getting the hitter to hit what they want him to hit.

The slider is probably as good a pitch as there is in baseball. All hitters have trouble with the slider; Mays says it's the toughest, Aaron says it's the toughest. I say it's the

greatest pitch in baseball. It's easy to learn. It's easy to control. Immediately, it gives a pitcher a third or fourth pitch for his repertoire.

The spitball is the biggest piece of fiction there is. They're always talking about the spitball. All a batter has to do is have the umpire look at the ball, because to be an effective spitter, the ball has to be loaded up good. I played under Frank Shellenback for two years in San Diego, the greatest spitballer in the minor leagues. He won three hundred games in the minors. He would have been in the majors if they hadn't outlawed the pitch. He threw spitters all the time, and I know he had to get the ball gobbered up with that slippery elm, and the more he got on it, the better it was.

You can't just wet your fingertips and throw a spitball. And you can't control it unless you throw it a lot. I defy any pitcher to show me he can do it just wetting his fingers. I hit against Lew Burdette. Everybody said he threw spitters. Maybe they were, but they didn't look like spitters to me. They'd sink, or fade a little. They certainly weren't *good* spitters.

Mike Garcia threw one at me one time, and the spit came up and hit me in the eye. The umpire threw the ball out. I didn't realize it, but Tommy Bridges said he threw one to me and I hit it out of the park.

As far as the fear hitters have of getting conked with the ball, all hitters go through it, and they must accept terror as a pitcher's legitimate weapon. A pitcher puts a hitter through those test periods. Start wearing down the fences and they start giving you a look, and then they find out if you can hit from the prone position.

I remember we had one pitcher on our club who Bill Skowron had been murdering, and the pitcher said, "Boy, the next time that Skowron gets up I'm going to hit him right on the NY"—right on the insignia of his cap. Bang, next time up he hit old Moose right on the helmet. It sounded like a cannon. I turned my head because I was sure he was badly hurt.

That's the second time I had done that. Don Buddin got hit with a ball one night when he was with the Red Sox. I was on the bench, and I turned away, and when I looked up both clubs had leaped out of the dugout and were on the field. Everybody out there but me.

A good hitter knows it's part of the act; the thing he must do as long as he plays is fight to stay in there, because once he starts bailing out, the pitcher has him beaten. I remember as a kid around the playgrounds in California, hearing the guys talking about beanballs, about scaring the batters, brushing them back, making them dance. I made up my mind way back then, "They aren't going to scare me."

Oh, I can't say I never had that little fear at the plate, especially in those early days when I'd be hitting against some guy who was a little out of my class. But I remember the time in Minneapolis, my third year as a professional, when a pitcher named Bill Zuber hit me in the head with a pitch. Knocked me out and put me in the hospital for two days. When I got back in the lineup, I dug in as hard as I could and said to myself, "Boy, this isn't going to stop me. Not a bit."

The Detroit staff always tried to give you a little fright—Benton, Trucks, Trout, Newhouser. They were always challenging you anyway, and they wanted to let you know they were in the park. But they were good pitchers who knew what they were doing. It's the guy who doesn't know where he's throwing who really bothers you.

Herb Score of Cleveland was considered to be a little on the wild side, but he didn't have a tough delivery. He was almost straight overhand, and with a guy throwing overhand the pitch is generally high or low. Score wasn't that wild anyway. He was on his way to being a great pitcher when he got hurt. A wild man who is *really* wild and throws more sidearm, or three-quarter arm, can make you hesitate.

I remember Ken Chase, who pitched for Washington. He had forearms like a milkman—he *was* a milkman, and still is. He had a hell of a curve. Hell of a fastball. But he was wild. It kept him from being a great pitcher. A wild man and an anteater. One day he got me to 3 and 2, with two men on, and threw a big sharp curve and I took it. Fooled me. Strike three. I got up again in the fourth inning, bases loaded, count goes to 3 and 2, and here comes another, and I'm hanging in there, waiting, waiting, and I don't think I moved until the ball was right by my ear. It hit my hat and spun it on my head.

Actually, pitchers seldom knocked me down, and Zuber was the only one who ever hit me on the head. When I first came up to Boston, they warned me to watch out for Johnny Allen; he had the reputation—"He'll low-bridge you, he'll knock you down"—but I got a couple hits off Allen the first time I faced him, and he never knocked me down. Early Wynn did, and Trout and Newhouser. I'm not sure it was intentional, but I have to think they could see no percentage in it. Newhouser knocked me down and struck me out that time, and I hit a home run next time up. Trout knocked me down, and I hit a home run on the next pitch. Same thing happened with Wynn.

As a manager, I certainly would not have my pitchers wasting their time knocking down hitters like DiMaggio, Greenberg, Foxx, Robinson, Joe Gordon, or Musial, or Lou Boudreau, or Al Kaline, because the only thing you do is rile them up. I would much prefer the pitcher try for the outside corner with a tough slider. Knock the guy down and you have wasted a pitch, and chances are when the batter gets up he'll be grinding.

I know there are hitters who can be intimidated, and pitchers who believe in keeping you loose. Jimmy Piersall told me he was afraid at the plate when he was with the Red Sox, and I tried to needle him out of it. "If you're afraid, you might as well go sell insurance. But why be afraid?" He worked himself out of it. His confidence grew. If you stay intimidated, you're done.

FOR PITCHERS: A THIRD PITCH

I didn't make a big thing about it, but I said when I took over the managership of the Senators in 1969 that I felt I could help not only the hitters but the pitchers, too. Nobody ever studied that little game between the hitter and the pitcher more than I did, so if I know hitting, I must know pitching. I started out as a pitcher, on the playgrounds of San Diego, was signed as a pitcher-outfielder, and even after I got to the big leagues I was exercised enough to get Joe Cronin to let me pitch a couple of innings against the Tigers one day.

But the main reason I think I know pitching is that I know what made it tough for me. Hitting is 50 percent from the neck up, and the most of what you learn concerns the pitcher.

I *know* that it's important for a pitcher to perfect his curveball. In only very rare cases will he get by on a fastball alone, no matter how good it is.

I *know* it's important to have that third pitch, the slider or a knuckleball. Immediately it gives the batter 33 percent more to worry about, a third alternative. The example I always use is the old shell game, where the guy is hiding a pea under three walnut shells. If he's got two, you can guess right 50 percent of the time without even looking. With three you're down to no better than 33 ½, and that's not good guessing.

I *know* it's important to make adjustments, to work to upset the batter's timing, to throw him off with a little different delivery, a little change in motion. I'm continually amazed how often pitchers don't know these things.

I don't say pitchers lack intelligence, but I do say most of them aren't smart about the game. They don't understand it as well as the players. How could they? They play once every five days. All they're interested in is throwing the ball—turning that hip, humping up, throwing the ball.

We had one pitcher on our Washington club who wanted to throw a fork ball all the time, and his curve hadn't improved. I told him he had to find something different. And he had to hump up and throw the ball. You can't lollipop it up there, trying to be fast and look good at the same time. There is nobody who throws hard throwing easy. The only way you can throw hard is to *throw hard*. Trying to look like you're throwing easy when you're throwing hard is bull. Get up there and grunt a little. That's the way to throw a fastball. Sam McDowell of the Indians has a helluva fastball, and I can hear him grunting all the way to the bench. He's putting something on it.

Very few pitchers know the game between the hitter and the pitcher, not the way a good hitter knows it. Very few know how to play certain hitters. They're not observant, partly because of their long activity lulls. Trial and error doesn't work on them as quickly. Watch Dwight Evans in the outfield. Enough balls start falling in front of him, he'll start shading the batter. Even if you're not extremely intelligent, these things make an impression

when you've played a team eighteen times. The pitcher is lucky if he gets in four of these eighteen games, so he doesn't bother to study.

Half the pitchers can't tell you why the ball curves, why it's important to grip it across the seams a certain way to improve the curve. It's simple enough: The more seams that spin in the direction of the pitch, the more resistance to the rotation of the pitch, the greater the curve. The curve itself ties in with Bernoulli's principle: As speed increases, pressure decreases.

What happens is this: Say the curveball is thrown 80 miles an hour. On a perfectly still day the resulting wind the ball passes through is equal to that speed (the same as the wind you hit when you stick your head out the window of a moving car). The wind goes on both sides of the spinning ball, but on the top side it is buffeted by the spin itself, slowing it down. The seams also work against it. On the bottom side, however, the speed is complemented by the spin of the ball. The result is a greater air speed on that side, and therefore less pressure, and that makes the ball drop or curve.

I have to laugh. We had a young pitcher on our staff who has as much stuff as anybody—Joe Coleman. I had him at my boys' camp in Lakeville, Massachusetts, when he was a teenager, and as I usually do, I told him what makes the ball curve, why it's not just an optical illusion, etc., etc. I told it to him twice.

I didn't see him again until the opening of spring training in 1969. One of the guys came to me the day Coleman arrived in camp. He said, "Ted, Coleman's worried."

"Yeah?"

"Yeah. Scared to death."

"Why?"

"He's afraid you're going to ask him what makes the ball curve. He says he knows how but still isn't sure why."

The biggest fault I find with pitchers is they don't adjust enough. They don't think with the hitter. They don't change their deliveries. It's so important, too. So important. I know Bobo Newsom used to give you that big windup, his arms flying around, and then, *whoom*, here comes the ball, and half the time you weren't set for it. He disturbed your concentration.

Johnny Allen used to change his delivery frequently. And Bob Lemon did it. What happened? Instead of that 15-inch square over the shoulder, the ball was coming from anywhere, and maybe the pitcher hesitated, or moved around on the rubber, or gave you another windup, another motion, a new tempo. Satchel Paige had about fifteen different deliveries. He was *always* changing that tempo.

I am sure much of the reason for Satchel Paige's fantastic longevity was that he threw the ball so many different ways. He had motion, he had control. He went through a stuff period when nobody had any more stuff. He went through a period where he was coy, and hesitating and could just mesmerize you. You'd watch all that and, *whoom*, he'd blow it past you.

Paige pitched until he was past fifty. I saw him first when I was a kid player in San Diego. There's no question he was one of the greatest, especially then. I hit against him four or five times and I kept saying to myself, "Boy, what a pitcher this guy must have been." I was impressed with his delivery, his easy, deceptive motion. All the time he was moving around on the mound, throwing from different angles, different windups. He'd stretch with the bases empty just to throw you off. He got me out every time that day.

Some pitchers are smart that way. If they're not getting you out, they'll change their motions, just naturally, and you see it and you think, "Gee, what is it?" and it's in on you before you know it. Pitchers should be told: Move around on the mound, try a little side-arm, change the tempo. Anything to upset that picture over the shoulder. Upset that and you upset the batter. If you've got two pitches and one delivery, you've got two pitches, period. Two pitches and *two* deliveries, that's *four* pitches.

Casey Cox had a real good year for the Senators in 1969. He had always struggled before that, but the talent was there. The only thing I asked Casey to do was to move around a little on the rubber: against right-hand batters, hedge a little bit toward the right side, give yourself a sharper angle for the curve; against left-handers, move back the other way.

As for that ability to think with the batter, most pitchers don't have it. I suppose in my experience the smartest two were Ted Lyons and Ed Lopat. Lyons had a great ability to cross you up, to be daring when you'd least expect it. You'd be thinking, "I know he's afraid to throw me this pitch," and he'd turn around and, umph, give it to you. He had that gift to figure you out and go the opposite way. Lopat was the same. Maybe even smarter. They were the best two reasons I know of for *not* guessing on the pitch.

But I'm not writing this to help pitchers. This is a hitter's guide. Pitchers don't pick up things very easily anyway. Half of them don't even take batting practice. And isn't it funny? The way the game is played they represent 11 percent of the team's batting lineup going into a game. They should be as much concerned about their hitting as anybody, especially during those four days between pitching assignments. I'd like to know how many games good-hitting pitchers like Warren Spahn, Early Wynn, Red Ruffing, and Bob Lemon won with base hits, or got the chance to stay in tight games in the late innings because they could hit.

A FEW WORDS ABOUT BUNTING

No one ever accused me of being a great bunter, so I wouldn't pretend to qualify as an instructor, but I will pass on a few things Nellie Fox once told me. Fox, who has since passed away, was one of our coaches at Washington. He was about the best bunter around when he played. I remember one year when he bunted safely—for *hits*—in 26 of 30 attempts. That's an .867 average. I'd take it any day. As

a manager, I developed a new interest in bunting because I had some pitchers who have cost us games because they couldn't bunt at an opportune moment.

Consider this—Nellie Fox talking:

Most hitters (certainly in a sacrifice situation) would prefer to bunt by squaring away to the pitcher before the delivery, but to bunt for a base hit it is better to launch the bunt from your regular stance.

For a right-hand hitter, this means sliding the right (or rear) foot back 10 to 12 inches in a kind of running-start position as the pitcher starts his windup. For the left-hander, the first move is a sharp pivot on the ball of the right foot, then a crossover step toward the pitcher with the left foot—literally a running start.

In either case, the top hand on the bat moves up to the trademark, the fingers holding the bat there as gingerly as possible. The thumb should be on the trademark (you ought to be able to feel it). "Feel" is very important. Doc Cramer used to make Fox carry a bat around as though it were a hot poker, with his thumb and forefingers as loose as possible. Fox says if Cramer suddenly tried to knock it out of his hands and couldn't he'd "kick my butt."

The top hand acts as a fulcrum; the bottom hand guides the direction of the bunt. The looseness of the top hand helps deaden the action of the ball. If, however, you are a right-hander trying to push the ball past the pitcher, or a left-hander dragging the ball, the opposite is correct: the top hand is held firmly so that the bunt can be sharply pushed.

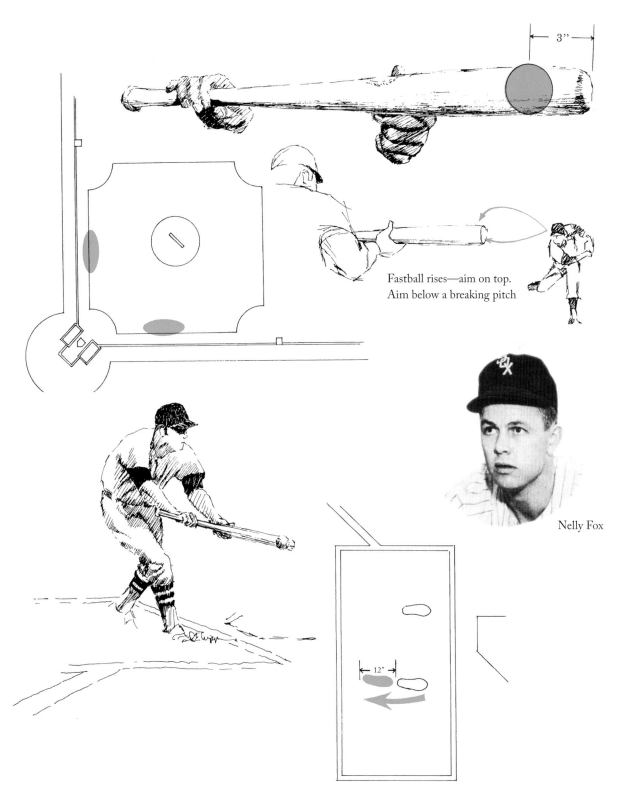

Fastball rises—aim on top.
Aim below a breaking pitch

Nelly Fox

3"

12"

Try to make contact with the ball on the last 3 inches of the bat. This will surprise a lot of guys who believe—and have preached—that you should bunt more toward the handle. The last 3 inches give a more deadening affect. Aim the bunt toward the outer edge of the grass along the baseline. (Circumstances may dictate a change in this, of course, but that spot is a good one for effective offensive bunting.)

Naturally, you bunt the top side of the ball to force it down on the ground, but here is another Foxism that may surprise you: A high ball is easier to bunt than a low ball. You don't have to angle the bat down and you can see the pitch better. Also, a fastball is easier to bunt than a breaking ball. With a fastball the rule is to stay on top; with a breaking ball, you must go down with it, you must bend more at the knees.

A left-hander has a distinct bunting advantage, of course, because he is two steps closer to first base from the start. But a right-hander can be as effective by paying attention to the situation and taking advantage. Is the third baseman back even with the bag, or maybe behind it? You can beat him with a good bunt. What's the count? What does the pitcher have to throw in this situation? Fox says a 1–0 pitch is a good pitch to bunt.

And, of course, practice. Practice in the batting cage, practice on the iron mike. Bunting isn't as easy as it looks.

PRACTICE, PRACTICE, PRACTICE

I don't think you can emphasize enough the importance of practice. When I say practice, I mean with a bat. In the spring that means hitting pepper, or down at the iron mike machine getting some extra licks, or just swinging a bat. As a kid I was *always* swinging a bat, an old Bill Terry model, pretending I was in the Polo Grounds, two outs, two strikes, two on, "Here's the pitch . . . *pow!*" another tremendous imaginary home run. Even as I got older, I'd have a bat handy all the time, a heavy bat to swing during the winter, something to fool around with under the coconut trees on the Florida Keys.

I know at my boy's baseball camp in Lakeville, I always got such a kick out of seeing a boy with talent, wanting to help him, wanting to be available to help him. I loved that. But if he didn't have the interest, if he wasn't willing to practice, to sacrifice, I didn't want to waste my time. I expect that now out of my players in Washington.

I think there are things you learn growing older in the game which practice brings out. You should, for example, never miss the ball in practice. You should always get a piece of it. If you're missing, something is radically wrong and you had better step out and think about it.

Chances are if it's that bad you will be in a slump, and slumps always follow a familiar pattern. When you first start going bad, you just try harder. Then you press, which means you do things unnaturally. Then you imagine you're getting all the tough breaks and you start feeling sorry for yourself.

It ought to be pretty nearly automatic what you do to straighten yourself out. Breaking a slump is very much the same as protecting yourself on a two-strike pitch. You start thinking in terms of going through the box. You make up your mind you're going to handle the bat better and you're not going to go after bad pitches or try to pull the ball. You're going to shorten up and be a little quicker.

As a manager at the big-league level, I've tried to do things that will help individuals while I'm helping the team. The dugout, for example, has always been a place in baseball where guys tended to doze. The very fact they're not playing works against them, so I try to keep them in the game: "What the hell pitch was that? What's the count?"

I'd see a guy check the scoreboard. "What are you looking there for? You oughta know without looking. Get in the game." "Two-zero pitch. Is he taking? What's he going to do?" The next time the guy'll notice. It's awful easy to daydream on the bench, so I'd give 'em that treatment. "Listen, you're lucky to be here. You could be in Denver, you know. You haven't got this club made. Let's have a little life."

My motive is straight enough: Today, even in the Little Leagues, platooning is a part of the game. You've got to keep sharp on the bench, because you're liable to be in there anytime. And platooning is really the only way to do it, unless you've got a stand-out player who's strong enough to play all the time. Otherwise there are forty different reasons to platoon *any* player. I don't mean a Robinson or a Powell or a Kaline, but listen—if you play eight guys all year and there are seven on the bench twiddling their thumbs, when you need them they can't do it because they haven't played.

We had Eddie Stroud pinch-hitting for the Senators, but I was always thinking of ways to get Stroud in the game. One pinch hit every other day isn't enough to keep you sharp; 100 pinch hits a year aren't enough; but if you can play twice a week, or once a week, and pinch-hit a couple times in between, then it's not completely foreign to you when you're sent in there. You're playing, you feel good, you win a game once in a while with an important hit—it gives you a little incentive, makes you want to practice more. But if you just sit a guy on the bench and leave him there, sooner or later he says, "Well, nuts to this outfit," and you can't blame him.

Listen. A .260 hitter can't hit .320. But if you can get that .260 hitter to hit .320 for a while, then you see him fade a bit and get him out of there, then back in when he's hot or against certain pitchers, give him an opportunity in the right situation, *boom,* he comes through, builds his confidence; and before you know it he isn't a .260 hitter, he's a .275 or a .280 hitter.

I think that every player should have goals, goals to keep his interest up over the long haul, goals that are realistic and that reflect improvement. For me, if I couldn't hit thirty-five home runs, I was unhappy. If I couldn't drive in 100 runs, if I couldn't hit at least .330, I was unhappy. Goals keep you on your toes, make you bear down, give you objectives at those times when you might otherwise be inclined to just go through the motions. You certainly cannot go through the motions and be a great hitter. Not even a good hitter. It's the most difficult thing to do in sport.

TED WILLIAM'S MINOR AND
MAJOR LEAGUE BATTING TOTALS

Year	Club	League	Pos.	G	AB	R	H	2B	3B	HR	RBI	BA
1936	San Diego	P.C.	OF	42	107	18	29	8	2	0	11	.271
1937	San Diego	P.C.	OF	138	454	66	132	24	2	23	98	.291
1938	Minneapolis	A.A.	OF	148	528	130°	193	30	9	43°	142°	.366°
1939	Boston	Amer.	OF	149	565	131	185	44	11	31	145°	.327°
1940	Boston	Amer.	OF–P	144	561	134°	193	43	14	23	113	.344
1941	Boston	Amer.	OF	143	456	135°	185	33	3	37°	120	.406°
1942	Boston	Amer.	OF	150	522	141°	186	34	5	36°	137°	.356°
1943–45	Boston	Amer.					(In military service)					
1946	Boston	Amer.	OF	150	514	142°	176	37	8	38	123	.342
1947	Boston	Amer.	OF	156	528	125°	181	40	9	32°	114°	.343°
1948	Boston	Amer.	OF	137	509	124	188	44°	3	25	127°	.369°
1949	Boston	Amer.	OF	155†	566	150°	194	39°	3	43°	159†	.343
1950	Boston‡	Amer.	OF	89	334	82	106	24	1	28	97	.317
1951	Boston	Amer.	OF	148	531	109	169	28	4	30	126	.318
1952	Boston§	Amer.	OF	6	10	2	4	0	1	1	3	.400
1953	Boston§	Amer.	OF	37	91	17	37	6	0	13	34	.407
1954	Boston	Amer.	OF	117	386	93	133	23	1	29	89	.345
1955	Boston	Amer.	OF	98	320	77	114	21	3	28	83	.356
1956	Boston	Amer.	OF	136	400	71	138	28	2	24	82	.345
1957	Boston	Amer.	OF	132	420	96	163	28	1	38	87	.388°
1958	Boston	Amer.	OF	129	411	81	135	23	2	26	85	.328°
1959	Boston	Amer.	OF	103	272	32	69	16	0	10	43	.254
1960	Boston	Amer.	OF	113	310	56	98	15	0	29	72	.316
	Major League Totals			2292	7706	1798	2654	525	71	521	1839	.344

° Led league
† Tied for lead
‡ Suffered fractured left elbow when he crashed into the left-field wall making catch in first inning of All-Star game at Chicago, July 11, 1950; despite injury he stayed in game until ninth inning. Williams had played seventy American League games up to the All-Star affair, but appeared in only nineteen more contests with the Red Sox for the rest of the season.
§ In military service most of the season

MY GALLERY OF GREAT HITTERS

AL SIMMONS: Known as "Bucketfoot" but had great power to all fields—Hall of Famer—Lifetime .334, mostly with Athletics—Led AL with .381 in 1930, .390 in 1931—AL MVP, 1929

BILL TERRY: Forsook power to hit for average—Consistently hit ball hard—Hall of Famer—Lifetime .341—Hit .401 for Giants to lead NL in 1930—Fine-fielding first baseman

TY COBB: (*above*) Smartest hitter of all—Hall of Famer—Highest lifetime average .367—Led AL hitters twelve times, nine in a row from 1907–1915, with Tigers—Slashing hitter, terrific speed afoot—Holds AL record for stolen bases, season (96), career (892)—Hit .420 in 1911, .410 in 1912—Played twenty-two years

MEL OTT: (*above*) Adapted style to park (Polo Grounds, NY) better than anybody (note foot in air)—Knew how to wait for pitch—Holds NL record for most bases on balls, 1,708—Hall of Famer—Lifetime .304 with 511 home runs—Led NL in homers six times with Giants

HARRY HEILMANN: (*right*) In my top five right-hand hitters of all time—Hall of Famer—Lifetime .342—Hit .403 for Tigers in 1923 and led AL three other years: 1921 (.394), 1925 (.393), 1927 (.398)—Told me he became great hitter when he learned to hit inside pitch to right field with two strikes

STAN MUSIAL: In my top five left-hand hitters of all time—Hall of Famer—Lifetime .331 with 475 home runs—NL batting champion seven times with Cardinals—Hit record five home runs in doubleheader, 1954—Holds lifetime total bases record (6,134), NL records for runs (1,949), hits (3,630), doubles (725), RBIs (1,949)—Voted NL MVP three times (1943, 1946, 1948)

JOE DIMAGGIO: The Yankee Clipper—In my five all-time right-handers—Great style, power, consistency—Hall of Famer—Lifetime .325 with 361 home runs—Twice AL batting champion, home run champion—Record of hitting safely in fifty-six consecutive games probably will never be broken—MVP three times (1939, 1941, 1947)

GEORGE SISLER: (*left*) Called "Gorgeous George"—People who saw him in prime say he may have been greatest player of all—Hall of Famer—Lifetime .340, mostly with old St. Louis Browns—Hit .407 in 1920, .420 in 1922—MVP, 1922

ARKY VAUGHAN: (*lower right*) Called "Arky" after home state of Arkansas—Fine-hitting shortstop with Pirates—Lifetime .318—Led NL in 1935 with .385, and in runs scored four times—MVP, 1935

CHUCK KLEIN: (*lower left*) Great left-hand power hitter—Lifetime .320 with 300 home runs—Led NL in homers four times with Phillies—Led NL batters with .368 in 1933—Set NL record for runs (158), 1930—MVP, 1932, 1933

ROGERS HORNSBY: The Rajah—Greatest right-hand hitter of all time—Hall of Famer—Lifetime .358 with 302 home runs—Led NL in batting seven times, six in a row from 1920–25, with Cardinals—Home run champion twice—Hit .400 three times: 1922 (.401), 1924 (.424), 1925 (.403)

TRIS SPEAKER: The Gray Eagle—Hall of Famer—Lifetime .344—Holds Major League record for outfield putouts, lifetime, 6,706; assists, 449—Led AL in doubles eight times, batting once (1915, .386), for Indians

SLUGGERS

JIMMY FOXX: (*top right*) In my top five right-hand hitters of all time—Great athlete, could do it all—Hall of Famer—Lifetime .325 with 524 home runs—Led AL in homers four times, three with Athletics, once with Red Sox—Hit 58 homers in 1932—Led AL in batting twice—Hit 30 or more homers twelve consecutive years, 1929–40—MVP, 1932, 1933, 1938

HACK WILSON: (*above*) Great home run power to opposite field—Lifetime .307, 244 home runs—Led NL in homers four times, with Cubs—Hit 56 homers in 1930, NL record—Drove in 190 runs, 1930

HANK GREENBERG: (*bottom right*) Smart hitter, always figuring with pitchers—Hall of Famer—Lifetime .313 with 331 home runs—Hit 58 homers for Tigers in 1938, led AL three other times—Led in RBIs four times—Hit two or more homers in eleven games, 1938, Major League record—MVP, 1935, 1940

BABE RUTH: Greatest power hitter of all—714 lifetime home runs, .342 average—Hall of Famer—Led AL in homers twelve times, eleven with Yankees—Led in RBIs six times—Led in batting, 1924 (.378)—Highest all-time slugging percentage, season, .847, 1920—Slugging leader record thirteen times—Record for runs scored, 177, 1921—MVP, 1923

LOU GEHRIG: In my top five left-hand hitters of all time—Iron Horse, played in record 2,130 consecutive games, Yankees, 1925–39—AL RBI record, season, 184 (1931)—Most bases-loaded home runs, lifetime (23)—Hall of Famer—Lifetime .340 with 493 home runs—Led AL batting, 1934; home run champion three times—MVP, 1927, 1931, 1934, 1936

RALPH KINER: Brief but brilliant career as power hitter—Led NL in home runs his first seven years with Pirates, 1946–52 (includes three ties)—Hit 8 home runs in four consecutive games, 1947, Major League record

MICKEY MANTLE: Greatest switch-hitting power hitter of all—AL home run champion, 1955 (37), 1956 (52), 1958 (42), 1960 (40)—Ranks fourth, all-time home runs, 536—MVP, 1956, 1957, 1962

JOHNNY MIZE: Most underrated of great hitters—Deserves to be in Hall of Fame—Lifetime .312, 359 home runs—NL batting champ, 1939 (.349), with Cardinals; NL home run leader twice for Cardinals, twice for Giants—RBI leader three times

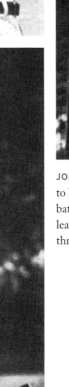

ROGER MARIS: Broke the record everybody said would never fall, Ruth's 60 home runs, by hitting 61 in 162 games, 1961, for Yankees—Never had a season like it before or after—MVP, 1960, 1961

AL KALINE: (*far left*) Only player to lead league in batting rookie season, 1955 (.340)—Lifetime .297 hitter with 399 home runs—Played twenty-two years with the Tigers without spending any time in the minor leagues

ERNIE BANKS: One of the best in baseball history at pulling pitch into power field. Lifetime .274 batting average with 512 home runs—100 or more RBIs seven times—Led NL, homers, 1958, 1960—MVP, 1958, 1959

HARMON KILLEBREW: A great power hitter .573 lifetime home runs—Homer champion, 1959 (42), 1962 (48), 1963 (45), 1964 (49), 1967 (44), 1969 (49)—RBI champ 1962 (126), 1969 (140), and 1971 (119)—MVP 1969

WILLIE MAYS: With Henry Aaron makes up my entry as fifth all-time best right-hand hitter. Tremendous power to all fields—660 lifetime homers third after Aaron and Ruth—2062 lifetime runs scored fifth on the all-time list—MVP, 1954, 1965

FRANK ROBINSON: A smart hitter who hit according to the situation. Lifetime .294, 586 home runs fourth on the all-time list—AL triple crown in 1966 (.316, 49 homers, 122 RBIs)—Only man to win MVP awards both leagues (with Reds, 1961; Orioles, 1966)

ROBERTO CLEMENTE: His tragic accident befell him at the peak of his powers. Extraordinary bat control and superb all-around player. His career ended with exactly 3,000 hits and a .317 lifetime batting average—NL batting champ, 1961 (.351), 1964 (.339), 1965 (.329), 1967 (.357), for Pirates—MVP, 1966

HENRY AARON: All-time home run leader with 755. One of baseball's smartest hitters ever—Great ability to get his pitch—Lifetime .305 batting average—Led NL in homers, 1957, 1966, 1967, for Braves—Drove in 100 or more runs eleven times—Batting champion, 1956 (.328), 1959 (.355)—MVP, 1957

PETE ROSE: With legendary hit 4,192 passed Ty Cobb and became number one on all-time hit list—Lifetime .300 average, with Reds, Phillies, Expos, and again the Reds—NL batting champion, 1968 (.335), 1969 (.348), and 1973 (.338)

MIKE SCHMIDT: Powerful hitter, excellent athlete. Gone through stages of moving around with—or being moved by—the pitchers. Big swing, much like Murphy. NL's MVP in 1980 and 1981; led in home runs six times (with a high of 48 in 1980) and in RBIs three times (121 in 1980)

ROD CAREW: Proven great ability to get the bat on the ball. Didn't hit with as much power as he was capable of, but why quibble? Led AL in batting seven times (high of .388 in 1977, but also an impressive .364 in 1974 and .359 in 1975). Pushing .333 lifetime. AL's MVP in 1977

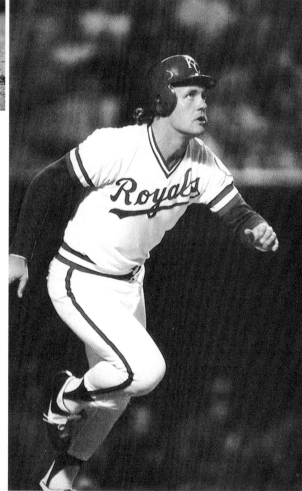

WADE BOGGS: Straightaway hitter, great ability to get the bat on the ball (à la Carew). Could hit more home runs (20 a year at least) if he extended himself because he gets the ball in the air. Doesn't realize yet how good he is (AL batting champion, 1983 (.361), 1985 (.368), 1986 (.357), 1987 (.363), and 1988 (.366). (Lifetime .328)

GEORGE BRETT: Got to think of him as 1–2–3, right at the top of the heap as the best hitter in baseball in the modern game. Knows the strike zone, makes good contact, seems to get stronger every year. AL's MVP in 1980 when he hit .390 (Lifetime .305)

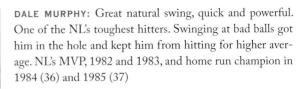

DALE MURPHY: Great natural swing, quick and powerful. One of the NL's toughest hitters. Swinging at bad balls got him in the hole and kept him from hitting for higher average. NL's MVP, 1982 and 1983, and home run champion in 1984 (36) and 1985 (37)

DON MATTINGLY: Stylish left-handed hitter; moved the ball around with good power, knew when to try to rip it. Led AL in hitting in 1984 (.343) and came close to triple crown in 1985 when he hit .324, had 34 home runs and led AL with 145 RBIs. Like Boggs, only four years in the big leagues, but already a star (Lifetime .307)

EDDIE MURRAY: Best switch-hitter of the medium game. Hit for average (always around .300) and distance (always around 30 home runs). Drove in more than 100 runs four times.

There are many current players in the MLB that are worthy of mention as a possible "Ted Favorite." The list below comprises a mix of age groups, length of service and achievement, but I'm sure Ted would have enjoyed watching them all play and probably would have had words of advice for each one of them.—JU

In no particular order:

Miguel Cabrera, Detroit Tigers

Derek Jeter, NY Yankees

Chipper Jones, Atlanta Braves

David Ortiz, Red Sox

Jim Thome, Baltimore Orioles

Josh Hamilton, Texas Rangers

Mike Trout, Los Angeles Angels

Ryan Braun, Milwaukee Brewers

Joey Votto, Cincinnati Reds

Ryan Howard, Philadelphia Phillies

Carlos Beltran, St. Louis Cardinals

David Wright, NY Mets

Alex Rodriguez, NY Yankees

Albert Pujols, LA Angels

Andrew McCutchen, Pittsburgh Pirates

Lance Berkman, Texas Rangers

Todd Helton, Colorado Rockies

Michael Young, Philadelphia Phillies

Matt Kemp, Los Angeles Dodgers

Ichiro Suzuki, NY Yankees

TED WILLIAMS: Named to Baseball Hall of Fame in 1966—Last of the .400 hitters, hit .406 in 1941—AL batting champion six times, home run champion four times—Holds Major League records for most consecutive playing years leading in runs scored (5), for most consecutive playing years leading in bases on balls (6), for most successive times reaching first base safely (16 in 1957), for most intentional bases on balls in a season (33 in 1957). Tied Major League record by hitting three home runs in a game twice during 1957; tied Major League record for most home runs in consecutive times at bat (4 in 1957) and tied AL record for most total bases in fewest consecutive times at bat (22, in eight times at bat, 1957). Led AL in total bases six times, in bases on balls eight times, in slugging percentage nine times—AL MVP in 1946, 1949—Hit .304 in 16 All-Star games and named Major League Player of the Decade by *The Sporting News, 1960*